# Unlocking Data Insights: Mastering Data Science for Impact

## Harnessing Big Data for Smarter Decisions

# Michael Lawson

# Table of Contents

# INTRODUCTION

In a data-driven world, people and institutions have the need to apply the power of data to make smarter decisions. This detailed guide, "Unlocking Data Insights: Mastering Data Science for Impact: Harnessing Big Data for Smarter Decisions," was designed to equip you with the skills and information you will need to succeed in this rapidly developing field of data science.

This book introduces the nexus of big data and data science in great detail, giving an accurate road map for comprehending, interpreting, and evaluating extremely vast datasets in the quest for useful insights. Whether a company leader, veteran data scientist, or simply a curious student, this book packs very insightful wisdom on using data to make a difference.

In addition to acquiring mastery in applying data science, machine learning, and big data technologies to real-world problems, you also explore the underlying notions behind these fields. The compass is hands-on, leading to simpler ways of making wiser decisions data collection, and cleaning to sophisticated engine learning models.

We focus on data being used ethically and on storytelling so that through that process, some innovation and change come along. When you finish reading this book, you will know exactly when and how to use data for your benefit so it can produce significant outcomes and affect your industry.

# CHAPTER I

# Data Science and Big Data

## The Evolution of Data Science

Data science, quite literally, at the confluence of computer science, statistics, and mathematics has become one of the most significant fields of the modern world in very quick time. Data science changed the way governments, corporations, and individuals make decisions from pure statistical analysis to big data analytics and its application with artificial intelligence. All these factors together have formed the basis of this development; specifically, the rise in the volume of data along with a growing realization about the fact that data could provide input toward enriching decision-making processes it offered has resulted in the emergence of data science as a discipline.

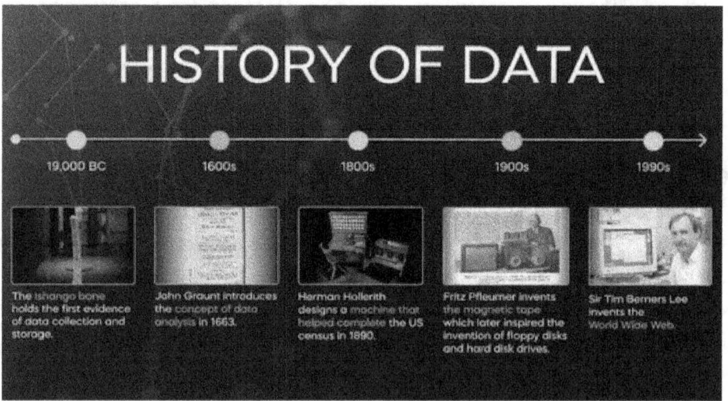



Well, data science as a discipline had a long history even before this term came into the picture. Early in the 20th century, the only method to analyze data was through statistical study. The pioneers like Ronald Fisher and Karl Pearson have mostly done the work of creating all the basic statistical techniques that have been in use today.

The early methods of interpretation were made possible through the work of Fisher on the significance of testing and the contribution of Pearson to correlation. These techniques mostly used to work on the data with tiny samples of economics, agriculture, and biology. At this point, researchers were mainly concerned with hypothesis testing which essentially necessitates the application of models in statistics to accept or reject assumptions pertaining to data.

The mid-20th century was another landmark when digital computers were discovered. Electronic processing of humongous data sets revolutionized this study area. The first databases were developed in the 1960s, which made it possible to store, retrieve, and alter data much more effectively than ever. In addition to creating the first databases, computer science also became an academically recognized field during this time; thus, with it, there would come the first hints of data science. Modern data science was first established when statisticians and computer scientists collaborated to create algorithms that could evaluate data at scale.

Improvements in processing power and storage capacity led to increasingly complex data analysis techniques in the 1970s and 1980s. RDBMS and personal computers made collecting, storing, and processing data at personal and organizational levels easy. Computer languages such as SAS and SPSS promoted further statistical analysis. Most attention was still focused on structured data, that is data aligned according to predetermined guidelines and was held in databases or spreadsheets. Rather than predicting what might eventually occur in the future, data analysis at this stage was largely descriptive, with analysts using the data in order to summarize what had happened before. The "data explosion," whereby companies began to generate and collect exponentially more data, started in the 1990s. Much of this was a result of the formation of the internet and the mass digitization of most elements of life. Largely unstructured quantities of text, images, and video erupted into forms of websites, social networks, and electronic transactions. The sheer amount and diversity of this data could no longer be approached by conventional statistical methods. Thus, new tools and instruments to deal with and assess unstructured data were invented during big data.

Very early in the new millennium, the term "data science" entered vogue to describe this novel form of data analysis, integrated into pieces of computer science, statistics, and domain-specific expertise. Some prominent statistician William S. Cleveland proposed in 2001 that there should be data science recognized as an independent discipline. He argued that the data science should be focused on how the data can be utilized for making decisions in multiple sectors, besides the respective processes of data collection and analysis. Once businesses recognized how data-informed insight can improve everything from a marketing plan to healthcare outcomes, this new concept of "data science" was quite widely embraced.

Machine learning, a subcategory of artificial intelligence that enables computers to find things out and learn from data without being explicitly programmed, gained traction mid-decade. Algorithms operating on big databases could start to draw patterns and even make predictions, and suddenly, a whole wave of possibilities opened up in data science. Because these algorithms could easily process huge volumes of data and give insights beyond the capability of humans, they were particularly well-suited to tackle big data. Machine learning thus became an important tool for the data scientist's toolkit with an entire gamut of applications, ranging from predictive analytics in banks to recommendation systems of e-commerce websites.

The area underwent a further transformation with the entry of big data technology such as Hadoop and Spark at the end of 2000, which helped businesses to process and measure their large datasets in a distributed computing environment that allowed data to be processed and stored in parallel across multiple workstations. With it, data scientists can now work on datasets which had been so unimaginably big by orders of magnitude impracticable to work on. It further made possible real-time data analysis such that organizations could make choices not only on past information but based on real-time data as well. The further shift toward real-time analytics thus solidified data science as a vital tool for corporate decision-making.

Data science proved to be one of the major driving forces of innovation in many industries in the 2010s. As social media, smartphones, and IoT will be omnipresent, data creation has never been out of control and is skyrocketing to new levels. Those businesses that have learned how to use data to their advantage in workflows have had a considerable edge over their competitors. Companies like Google, Amazon, and Facebook have grown to be among the world's most valuable because of its ability to leverage data science in the improvement of processes and tailoring offerings. While public policy, education, and healthcare have also mastered data science methods to their own advantage by pushing through breakthroughs in personalized learning, medical research, and evidence-based policymaking.

Among these, the first and foremost trend is the rising automation in data science. Most of those processes that traditionally required the knowledge of a data scientist, such as feature selection and model tweaking, can now be automated with the assistance of AutoML, or automatic machine learning tools. Another trend is the increasing importance of explainable AI. As models get more complex, it becomes increasingly difficult for humans to understand how machine learning models are actually making decisions. One of the "black box" issues raises concerns over the accountability and transparency of AI systems, especially when these systems have been employed in high-stakes fields like criminal justice, healthcare, and finance. In this regard, scientists work on explainable AI approaches intended for bettering the transparency and interpretability in machine learning models' decision-making processes.

Finally, it seems that data science will be married up to disciplines. As data science continues to mature, increasingly it has been getting married up with domain-specific knowledge to tackle more complex problems. Data science has been applied in precision medicine to analyze genetic data and develop individualized treatment plans. Data science is being applied to environmental research to model climate change and develop mitigation strategies. This trend toward interdisciplinary collaboration is bound to accelerate as volumes and complexities of data increase.

Data science has come a long way from when it was first developed out of statistics to its position today as one of the driving forces behind innovation in the age of digital technology. Technological developments, expansion of big data across the globe, and increased recognition of the need for data-driven insights have majorly influenced the area. Despite the presence of challenges such as moral dilemmas and the need for improvement of data literacy, the future of data science indeed appears bright. New tools and techniques will continue changing sectors, driving innovation and possibly helping solve some of the world's most crucial problems in data science.

## Define Data Science and Big Data

Data science and big data have been considered two of the most revolutionary ideas of the twenty-first century: engines driving scientific success, economic growth, and technological innovation. Yet their names are used almost interchangeably, although they point to two very different concepts. Big data represents the enormous amounts of structured and unstructured data that are produced on an unprecedented scale, while data science is concerned with the strategies, processes, and systems used to assess and interpret large volumes of data. To understand their roles in the modern world, one ought to understand how the two differ from each other and how they relate with each other. The section will explore the features, applications, and the way data science and big data transform several industries to clearly define them.

Fundamentally, data science is a multidisciplinary field that applies scientific systems, algorithms, and methods to extract knowledge and insights from data. Therefore, it has drawn elements from some other fields, including computer science, statistics, mathematics, and domain knowledge. Data science can be said to deal with complex data on the real-world problem issues and means the interpretation of it. It is, therefore, a very broad field: ranging from highly advanced techniques like machine learning and artificial intelligence to simple operations like data cleansing and processing. This is because there are many applications that are different yet effective in drawing conclusions from data, useful information delivery, and decision-making in various organizations.

Data science collect information and organizes the data. The knowledge can exist from any source: a public database of readings from sensors, social media posts, or business transactions. Any data science effort starts with the step of preparing and cleaning the data to ensure its quality. Data scientists have to work on standardization and arrangement of the data, which is often erroneous, in many places duplicated, and consists of missing information, even before actual analysis can be done. This is indeed an important stage as the quality of the input data determines the accuracy and reliability of the results that will be generated. After data is prepared in this way, data scientists use multiple statistical techniques and machine learning algorithms to analyze that data. Output or classification based on predictions can be developed with the training of machine learning models by using past data; statistical techniques help find relations and patterns in the data. For instance, through data science, buyers will be able to predict which products the purchaser is going to buy according to the routine of their previous investments. This learning assists businesses in creating optimally working processes and drawing conclusions from data and providing consumer experiences in a more bespoke way.

Data science also contains other areas of data science, such as data visualization and communication. One of the big challenges in this domain is that results from data analysis are not easily understandable and especially for nontechnological stakeholders or communication. Data scientists can utilize the right data visualization tool or transform complex data into an aesthetically pleasing form: interactive dashboards, graphs, or charts. These are all vital in transforming data into a story so that decision-makers will not be left behind, knowing the importance of the findings for them to take action appropriately. Of course, without applied methodology, the most advanced study is only meaningless.

Another very important feature of data science is how it implements AI and machine learning in the science of data. Machine learning-one branch of AI-allows systems to learn about data and make judgments or projections without having specifically been programmed to do so. Data science employs various kinds of machine learning models in order to classify data, establish trends, and project into the future. Such models can be unsupervised, which detect hidden structures in data without any labeled outcomes or supervised, which are trained on labeled data to provide predictions. An example would be using unsupervised learning algorithms in consumer segmentation, where companies can determine several groups of customers according to the purchasing patterns.

The growing importance of data science can be traced back to the rise of big data. Big data is a term that gives a name to the vast amounts of information generated today in the digital world at a never-before-seen scale and velocity. There are five essential characteristics that define it: volume, variety, rapidity, veracity, and value. The term "volume" describes the total amount of data, which can be anything from terabytes to petabytes. Variety represents the different types of data that might be present, including unstructured data, such as text, pictures, and videos; semi-structured data, like XML files; and structured data, for instance in a database format. Veracity defines the correctness and reliability of the data, while velocity is the speed at which it generates data and processes it. Value is the perceived benefit and understanding that may come out of the data.

Big data originates from numerous sources, such as mobile devices, transactional records, social media, and sensors. For instance, the billions of discussions, comments, and uploads that happen daily on platforms such as Facebook and Twitter constitute enormous data. Similarly, data obtained in the healthcare industries by analyzing equipment used and electronic health records can be continually gathered and can be used to inform and improve patient results. More devices will connect to the Internet of Things, increasing the volume and variety of data. This is a challenge but at the same time, an opportunity for data scientists to come up with solutions.

Big data has difficulty in organizing and storing huge datasets and more so, in coming up with effective ways to efficiently evaluate such data. Traditional analytical methods are inapplicable when it comes to processing big data due to its size and complexity. Data science kicks in at this point with greater relevance as it relates to issues of machine learning and artificial intelligence. The sophisticated use of algorithms and distributed computing platforms like Hadoop and Spark enables the examination of large loads of data through data scientists to highlight patterns, trends, and correlations that might be less straightforward to trace with other methods.

Its main utilization, however, is predictive analytics, by forecasting future events or actions based on data. Finance big data analytics provides all the tools to forecast market trends and direct investment plans. Big data, or better known as predictive models, can enhance treatment strategies in health care, stop the occurrence of disease outbreaks, and predict patient outcomes. It is helpful in predicting consumer preference and improving advertising strategies by marketing organizations. The ability of an organization to predict the outcome of something based on previous data places them in a convenient competitive position to be proactive rather than reactive.

Real-time analytics is another advantage of big data, which allows organizations to make choices not based on history but on the current. For instance, financial institutions can use real-time data analysis to detect fraud transactions in time to prevent them from being done. Retailers can offer personalized offers or dynamically change their inventories in real-time by monitoring customer behavior. Social networks will analyze real-time activity to suggest content, identify trending topics, and direct conversations. Thus, real-time analytics will be very valuable in sectors like finance, healthcare, and telecommunications, where people need to respond at any given moment.

Big data use is not without issues, though. There are primarily two problems: security and privacy of data. The more private information that organizations collect regarding people, the higher the likelihood of misuse or unauthorized access to this confidential information. Data breaches may cause severe damage to a person's reputation, lead to financial losses, and even be the legal basis for both persons and companies. Governments and regulatory bodies responded to the thinking with enactment of data protection laws such as the General Data Protection Regulation of the European Union that spells out standards on gathering, storing, and processing personal data. Organizations seeking to tap into big data in non-breaching ways of privacy standards have to be compliant with these standards.

The issue with data quality is yet another challenge associated with the use of large data. Big data sets generally contain a lot of unstructured data, which might be disorganized, erroneous, or incomplete. Such low-quality data can lead to wrong conclusions and analysis. In order to make sure that the data being analyzed is valid, therefore, data scientists must embrace strong data cleaning and preprocessing techniques. This will imply standardizing formats of data, eliminating duplicates, and filling up missing values. Data quality is very important in key decisions like deciding the outcome of a financial transaction or diagnosing a medical condition. The development of big data has raised new ethical concerns, too. Bias and fairness have been some particular concerns over the use of big data in AI systems. This further implies that biased datasets used to train AI models can perpetuate or even exacerbate already-existing disparities. Algorithms of bias, especially for sentencing and policing methods, can be the result; this is particularly worrisome for areas such as criminal justice.

Thus, the need for ethical standards and responsibility in the applications of AI and big data has lately become visible. However, apart from fighting to reduce bias and discrimination in their models, data scientists and organizations are responsible for being transparent about how data is collected and used.

In a nutshell, one can say that big data and data science are subjects that are forcefully intertwined, changing the face of society, politics, and business. Big data is the term used for the vast amounts of information generated in today's digital world; data science is the area providing techniques as well as resources that enable an assessment of the understanding about the data. When combined, they help business enterprises come up with new ideas, forecast future trends, and gain insights. However, with big data arises issues of data integrity, privacy, and ethics. Big data and data science will be the big players as the technology rolls out, holding immense potential to change an entire industry or solve some of the biggest problems that plague the face of humanity. Anyone hoping to navigate this emerging data-driven future must first understand the foundations of both big data and data science.

## Data Science in Modern Decision-Making

Decisions in this data-intensive, high-networked world are no longer instinctive or based on fuzzy knowledge. Instead, they are increasingly getting powered by a burgeoning field of science data -- a multidisciplinary field combining methods from computer science, statistics, and domain-specific knowledge to draw useful insights from enormous datasets. Data science has enabled companies to make more informed decisions, encouraging productivity, better performance, and, in the first place, an edge over the rest of the markets. This section focuses on how data science functions operate when it comes to modern decision-making, rising importance in most industries, and a revolutionary impact on both businesses and society at large.

Put, data science is a solution to problems and answering with the help of data. The last few years have witnessed rapid growth in data from social media activity, online transactions, and information captured by the sensors. This has opened doors to new ways of gaining insightful information for organizations. This process is made easier by data science by providing a structure for gathering, organizing, assessing, and then making sense of the data. This allows raw data to be transformed into insights that may assist in decision-making in almost any area; these include public policy, healthcare, and commercial strategy and marketing.

Data science enhances the quality of a firm's decisions primarily by means of predictive analytics. This helps organizations make proactive instead of reactive decisions in the light of available past data predicting what might probably happen with respect to events, trends, or behaviors. Predictive analytics can be used to predict revenues, manage inventories, and predict client preferences. Using data science models, an e-commerce company can predict which products will be in most demand over the next few months. This way, it can stock up or scale down appropriately based on those predictions. Predictive models are also used in finance to help an organization better identify risks and alter strategies in order to minimize those threats, be it a change in the market or clients falling into loan default.

Personalization is one of the most significant applications of data science to inform decisions. Consumers now expect customized experiences in this digital age of consumerism as they shop online, stream media, or click on content on social media. Data science enables firms to make their service adjusts to taste at the individual level based on the analysis of consumer behavior and preference. For example, Netflix and Spotify are streaming services that use algorithms to make recommendations for content based on what a user has done or their past choices. Such platforms could offer user enjoyment and improved engagements at a very tailored level through an assessment of a view or listening behavior.

Data science is pertinent to business operations as it ensures streamlined processes and greater productivity. Through data analysis of the processes involved in running operations, businesses will identify what needs improvement or even inefficiencies and bottlenecks. A good example can be seen in data science-based real-time monitoring of production lines within the manufacturing industry. Thus, a manager will identify the problem before it becomes significant enough, reducing downtime and increasing output. For example, data science models can be applied in an effort to enhance logistics and supply chain management with regard to inventory control, optimization of delivery routes, and the prediction of change in demand. It also facilitates the smoothing of operations and maximizes resource usage for increased profitability.

Data science is changing decision-making outside the commercial sector toward education, public policy, and even health care. Data science application in the health sector provides better patient outcomes through more accurate diagnoses and tailored treatments. For instance, predictive models may be applied by doctors to point out which individuals are at a higher risk of contracting various diseases such as diabetes or heart disease, hence early intervention. Precision medicine is another area of application for data science. Here, the genetic data are analyzed with a view to designing a specific type of therapeutic plan suiting every patient. Such improvements in data-driven healthcare led to the progress of diseases from turning into one's reversals, thereby averting useless treatments and also improving the results of patients without increasing healthcare costs.

Data science enables the educational institutions to increase students' and result of learning satisfactions. Data analysis on the performance of students shall reveal those in danger and offer them specific interventions towards their achievement of desired outcomes. For instance, learning analytics solutions can provide personalized learning pathways that adapt both the content and the pace of instruction to individual needs through statistics on participation, attendance, or performance. The above data-driven approach in education empowers better academic results and more effective teaching techniques. It is also generally impacting the process of making public policy decisions. Governments and other institutions increasingly use data to measure the success of programs, allocate resources, and influence various policy decisions. The public services of a city can be better managed through data analytics to optimize the flow of traffic, improve garbage collection, and reduce energy consumption. Data science helps police and law enforcement agencies identify trends in criminal activities, and this allows them to resource allocation better and halt criminal activity. Data-driven policymaking results in an efficient and fair outcome since judgments would be based on factual evidence rather than political or personal prejudices.

One of the main reasons why data science is as relevant as it is in the decision-making processes of today is because with the technology and highly sophisticated tools used, it's now possible to process tremendous volumes of data. As big data platforms, cloud computing, and various techniques in machine learning continue to make things possible that had before been inconceivable with the analysis of large data sizes, so is it now feasible to process and store petabytes of data through various big data technologies like Hadoop and Spark and, what's more, teamwork in geographically separate teams on real-time analytics is now made possible through cloud platforms. This is also allowing the machines to discover patterns that are hidden in the data but could not be found by humans. It makes it possible for businesses to produce forecasts and predictions which may be potentially more accurate than what they are accustomed to. Benefits of using data science when making decisions are self-evident, but risks associated with data science when making decisions are numerous. One major problem this comes with is the quality of data acquired. Data about misinformation or wrong or outdated facts might lead to incorrect inferences and the wrong choice making. With this, data scientists need to follow stiff processes of cleansing and validating data to ensure that analyzed data is credible. The need is even more urgent in sectors like finance and health care in which the deadly aftereffects of poor choices dominate.

Another issue with data-driven decisions is that it is possible to have bias in choice-making. It's because as good as the training data, machine learning models are that the very racial, gender, or socioeconomic biases may thus be manifested or even amplified by the models themselves. Of course, this has made a huge hue and cry, especially within areas where biased algorithms would result in unfair or discriminatory outcomes, such as lending and hiring, not to mention law enforcement. Companies must establish norms to use data and data responsibly scientists must be ahead in the process of discovery and removal of bias from their models. Data privacy is the largest concern in data-driven decision making. The more collection the organization does on personal data, the higher the chances that it can misuse or sell illegal access. Sensitive information needs attention from all of its stakeholders, especially after the most publicized cases of data breaches brought this real problem to the spotlight. Organizations require such law just like GDPR to make sure that people's privacies are well protected and otherwise if they do not want to incur such losses and suffering, then they need to ensure compliance with such standards and thus be very strong in security measures. It should also enable individuals to have control over their personal data, and the processes relating to the methods of such data collection and usage are made transparent and intelligible, seeking consent every time.

While such formidable challenges exist, still huge scope does exist for the alterative of decision-making by data science. One of the most interesting topics that are currently under development is machine learning and artificial intelligence applied towards automated decision making. The systems can process large volumes of data on real time, but more interestingly, become a basis for decision-making acts without human input. For instance, for an AI trading system in finance, it can carry out trades based on real-time feeds of optimized methods that maximize returns. An AI-driven robotics system where a determination of its production cycles can be made concerning methods that yield maximum productivity with maximum waste elimination. More benefits are associated with automated decision-making; however, more challenging moral and legal issues arise. For example, in case an AI goes wrong and hurts people, who is going to bear the blame? How can we ensure that automated decision-making is just and transparent? As more applications of AI in decision-making come under development, the scope for understanding frameworks that make procedures directed by AI just, accountable, and transparent has also increased. Research and legislature formulate policies and regulations to ensure AI is used appropriately and ethically.

In short, data science is gaining momentum in each sector of the economy, either it is about taking decisions or even creating more and more advanced things. Data science gives business the opportunity of evaluation and understanding of enormous volumes of data, hence giving them knowledge and experience required to make better, fact-based decisions. Applications of data science are broad-ranging and transformative, ranging from personalization and predictive analytics to operations optimization and public policy. Organizations will need to address questions of data quality, bias, privacy, and ethics as data science increasingly forms an integral part of decisions that support those goals. That way, data science will help maximize all the potential it holds to increase creativity, output, and more just and sensible decisions.

Of course, those decisions are going to be ever more subject to the advanced infidelity of increasingly complex technology in data science and artificial intelligence and machine learning. The more intricate the technologies become, the more complicated things they are going to have to analyze, therefore allowing companies to spot patterns, minimize inefficiencies, and react with unprecedented precision and swiftness to challenges. Companies that are going to pivot on data science and related innovations will probably have a better chance of facing this already perilous and data-dependent future.

## Key Players and Tools in Data Science

Data science is a field that amalgamates aspects of statistics and mathematics, together with the vast branch of computer science, for valuable insights from the mammoth databases. All this has become increasingly significant in industrial developments, decision-making, and innovations concerning areas like technology, healthcare, finance, and education. The actors who spearhead the evolution of the field of data science are referred to as major players, while those tools supporting work engaged in data science by the data scientist so that they can easily process, analyze, and visualize data are called tools. This section discusses the major players and tools of data science. It brings out the contribution of each of the major players to the field as well as the role of each tool in shaping the future of data-driven decision making.

The first notable icon of data science is the data scientist. A data scientist is a professional who derives insights using data. Data scientists have a particular set of abilities - they know their domain, have programming expertise, and should be able to reason mathematically. A good data scientist is very well aware of the context in which the company or industry operates and has skills that deal with data analysis, machine learning, and data visualization. Data scientists have the onus of giving a data-driven answer to difficult problems from the problem-solver's desk. Data scientists are responsible for scanning massive datasets to clean up and preprocess them, apply machine learning models, and interpret the outcome to ensure valid recommendations in banking, health, retail, or any other domain.

The second essential player in data science is the data engineer. They guarantee availability, structure, and preparation of the data for analytical use, while data scientists actually work with the data and analyze it. They create and design the infrastructure in terms of necessary and effective processing and storage of data. The data engineers create pipelines such that the transfer is smooth from multiple sources to the data scientist. It is only possible to access and process the massive amounts of data required by a data scientist with the aid of data engineers. Furthermore, data engineers have a critical role to play in that the data systems they design have to be scalable and reliable, especially when enterprise companies begin producing and storing high amounts of data.

The second crucial element of the data science ecosystem is the machine learning engineers. Machine learning falls under the category of artificial intelligence, which enables systems with the capability to learn from data and make judgments or predictions without explicit programming. A group of machine learning engineers develops, tests, and applies the models in recognition patterns, classification of data, and predictions. Often, these machine learning engineers cooperate closely with other collaborating data scientists who work together to engineer algorithms in order to automate a variety of decisions. A machine learning engineer may design a model that could detect fraudulent transactions for a financial services firm or predict client churn in some subscription industry. Machine learning engineers' onus lies in the fact that such models should work well, be scalable, and can be easily integrated into production systems.

Data science plays an equal role for business analysts, too. Where business analysts translate the insights about data to the context of business strategy, the nitty-gritty of the data analysis goes into the domain of the data scientist. A business analyst bridges the gaps between technical teams and decision-makers, to ensure that data-driven insights are actionable in line with what business needs are. Business analysts tend to make frequent use of data visualization tools when trying to communicate their findings to business executives in a way that's easy for them to understand. A business analyst helps an organization make strategic, effective use of data to analyze performance and spot trends. For instance, for data information that concerns a marketing campaign, one can give advice on changes or based on performance metrics, changes in the operation.

Domain experts can be supported in data science. Domain experts work with data scientists to ensure that any analysis carried out on the data is relevant and applicable. What is the value in bringing that kind of domain knowledge into it? That is extremely deep understanding in some business or space-health care, finance, or maybe retail. Even though they possess fantastic technical skills, data scientists may need to gain the specialized industry knowledge that will make them understand the data they are playing with. The gap is thus filled by domain experts, as they provide context and guidance on what questions are to be asked and how to interpret results. A domain expert in health care includes a doctor who will collaborate with data scientists to analyze patient data and develop predictive models for disease diagnosis. Their knowledge ensures that solutions based on data are sound technically and relevant for real-world applications.

On the organizational level, some of the largest technology companies also play a crucial role in the evolution and maturation of data science. Innovators in data science include Google, Microsoft, and Amazon; they have developed the platforms, research, and tools that enable data-driven decision making all over the world. For instance, some of the most sophisticated algorithms related to machine learning have been developed by it, and this is complemented by data processing, analysis, and storage through its platform known as Google Cloud Platform. The other strong contender has been Microsoft, through its Azure platform offering cloud-based solutions on artificial intelligence, machine learning, and big data analytics. Another noteworthy one is Amazon Web capabilities, or AWS: for instance, powering advanced analytics and machine learning capabilities which can drive data science initiatives, as well as scalable computing and storage solutions.

Other important elements of the data science ecosystem include the open-source community. Data scientists and developers collaborate, share code, and leverage each other's work across GitHub and similar forums. Effort in data analysis and machine learning brought on the open-source library revolution in data science in the forms of

TensorFlow, PyTorch, and Scikit-learn, where the data scientist develops complex models while conducting profound analysis, not needing to start anew. The open-source ecosystem helps to promote innovation by making the most recent developments in data science more accessible to a broad audience via cooperation and knowledge exchange.

Now, let's talk about the tools which bring data science to life. By major players covered, now it is time talking about the tools making data science happen. Programming languages are basically the most important tools in data science. Generally, the programming language used in the field of data science is Python, mainly for its simplicity and flexibility with extensive libraries and framework ecosystems. Library needs for computation and numerical analysis include NumPy and Pandas. Matplotlib and Seaborn are essential tools for visualization purposes. Much of the current hype in Python is related to good support by a large community and relatively easy-to-read syntax, thus it's an equally terrific language for beginners and seasoned data scientists alike.

Another popular programming language in data science is R, especially in higher education and research. R becomes the preferred tool for statisticians and data analysts performing extensive statistical modeling because of its robust skills regarding statistical analysis. The tool is useful to the data scientist carrying out statistical research and exploration because of its wide selection of packages for statistical analysis, machine learning, and data visualization. These allow for the storage of structured data, thus enabling easy retrieval and query ability. For these reasons, relational databases are very common among most data scientists for data processing and storage. Big data technologies, such as Apache Hadoop and Apache Spark, are used in handling large-scale unstructured data. It then has the features of Hadoop that allows big data processing and storage in a distributed manner whereas Spark facilitates much faster data processing in terms of memory compared to the earlier approaches.

Another tool that is highly used in Data Science is data visualization, which would enable the data scientists to report on findings in simple ways and convincingly. Many efforts are given in the creation of interactive dashboards and reports for stakeholders, where they can look at data from a visual perspective with the help of tools like Tableau and Power BI. This is because it allows organizations to develop data-driven decisions that are founded on visual insights by enabling data scientists and business analysts to picture complicated data in a way that is easily understandable to a non-technical person. Besides these basic tools, technologies for machine learning and artificial intelligence are a must have in the data science field. Among the most widely used open-source libraries for designing machine learning models, TensorFlow initiated by Google stands out. It has widely been used on working on neural networks, image identification, and natural language processing. The other library with great power is PyTorch, which is developed by Facebook. It is particularly popular for its flexibility and ease of use. All this helps a data scientist to develop, tune, and deploy a machine learning model that can exhibit the full gamut of a suggestion engine, predictive analytics, and regression and classification.

Cloud computing service providers like Google Cloud, Microsoft Azure, and AWS offer scalable infrastructure for processing, analyzing, and storing data. Such systems deliver real-time analytics, data warehousing, machine learning, and all types of data science services. That enables business applications to carry out sophisticated analysis and store huge volumes of data, without occupying hardware space. In such exponential growth of volume, scalability becomes very important. The best thing about these cloud platforms is that they're all about collaborations; hence, one can use tools that allow data scientists to collaborate on any project located anywhere in this world.

Amongst the important aspects of the data science industry, collaboration and version control stand out particularly when in big projects. Data scientists can share code in addition to working together on various versions of projects while following all changes using an application like Git and GitHub. With this, data science teams can collaborate flawlessly while developing complex multi-dimensional projects with many contributors. The aftermath of artificial intelligence and machine learning is also the development of specialized hardware, such as Graphics Processing Units (GPUs) and Tensor Processing Units (TPUs), that supposedly speed up the processing of a variety of computations necessary in machine learning. These pieces of hardware enable data scientists to train much more complicated algorithms and to work on much bigger datasets far much faster. Especially in deep understanding, it is extremely important in which GPUs and TPUs are included, considering the massive neural networks, which most probably use intense processing for effective training.

To say it in a nutshell, this advancement in data science and its usage come along with the principal influencers and resources of this domain. Data scientists, data engineers, machine learning engineers, business analysts, and domain specialists all contribute to extracting insights from data into actionable plans. The trade tools provide infrastructures and capabilities that make data science happen- a ladder of sorts, elevating up from big data technologies such as Hadoop and Spark to programming languages like Python and R. What will decide the further maturity of data science is how technology will continue to advance ever more sophisticated technologies and the collaboration of critical agents that will shape the future of data-driven decision-making globally.

## Ethics in Data Science

The increasing usage and influence across industries in data science are therefore raising interest in ethical dilemmas concerning the use of data science. Data science broadly encompasses very large-scale data gathering, analysis, and interpretation. This implies that numerous issues face data science, such as issues of privacy, bias, justice, and accountability, but also a tremendous potential for groundbreaking discoveries and insights. The importance of ethics to data science requires more focus on it for the reason that decisions in data science have a big impact not only on the individual but also on the society. The section discusses the significance of ethics in data science, the challenges of data scientists, and the frameworks that result in good moral behavior.

The core of all the ethical issues that data science faces includes a privacy issue. There is growing concern over the storage, sharing, and utilization of the volumes of sensitive and personal data that businesses gather. Individuals' behaviors, tastes, health, and financial information are some of the sensitive data that can be exploited in forming complex profiles at the risk of abuse or injury. It is in this context, then, that privacy rights go wrong if applied or handled wrong, and serious these implications are discrimination, identity theft, and a loss of public confidence in an organization. It then falls to the data scientist to work within the limits of the principles of consent and openness. This is making people know how their data is being used, and then there is a giving of powers to limit the exploitation of their data.

Data security is a matter of ethics because the data is stored electronically and thus are exposed to hacking, breaches, and unauthorized access. The last few years have seen scandals in breaches of data where hundreds of millions of people have been affected and handed over personal information to hostile actors. Beyond damaging specific persons, these breaches give way to a decline in public confidence in the companies handling and holding their data. Data scientists hence have to ensure data security as paramount and have robust safeguards against theft, unauthorized access, and misuse of data. This includes protection through encryption, safe storage, and routinely tracking systems to find security flaws. They also have to abide by data protection laws, like GDPR in Europe, which enforces the management and security of personal data under stringent conditions.

Bias is one of the major ethical issues present in data science. Data is considered unbiased and objective. However, it may help illustrate the bias and the prejudices of society because of how such biases could appear in the algorithms used to analyze the data, in the data itself, or in the choices made in response to the analysis. For example, since the data used to train the machine learning algorithms is likely to contain examples of discrimination prior to the present time, this further entrenches the status quo. Demeaning outcomes may even arise in employment, credit, or law enforcement. For example, an application in hiring practice used may favor males more than females depending on training that the application has gotten based on biased past data with regard to gender. Similarly, a lending model that has fed into biased credit information will deny loans to some groups of people.

Each stage of the process needs careful assessment in dealing with bias in data science. In this regard, data scientists should thus take extreme care in identifying and minimizing the bias those models they build, and their decisions harbor. This entails cleaning and preparing the data for removing biases and using algorithms conscious of fairness as well as thorough testing on the models to ensure that they do not produce discriminatory results. More to this, data scientists should understand that ethical considerations always require conscious thinking and examination and that bias sometimes cannot be measured or visible.

Data science ethics comprise fairness as well as other elements of bias. For a data science model and algorithm to be fair, it must treat the subject as well as all groups fairly without fostering bias in support of one group at the expense of others. Since fairness is a pretty vague and relative concept, it is virtually impossible to warrant. There exist several definitions of fairness, hence what might be taken as fair in one given case may not be so for another. For instance, although the algorithm used in predictive policing would likely make true predictions about crime trends if implemented with the use of input from prior data, it would only end up victimizing minority communities because the algorithm would decide the areas that have the highest rates of crime. A prioritization model in the healthcare sector that gives precedence to a patient over others for specific risk factors may inadvertently discriminate against vulnerable patients who lack an easy and convenient means of accessing care.

These issues need comprehensive context-sensitive analysis and take into account various stakeholders in making decisions towards solving the moral dilemma. It demands that data scientists engage with ethicists, lawyers, and community leaders so that models aren't in conflict with principles of justice and fairness. Data scientists are also expected to be transparent and truthful about the bound limitations of the model developed, which indicates the potential for possible biasing or unconscious impacts on findings.

The other important component of ethical considerations in data science is accountability. This makes mechanisms for accountability more crucial with the inclusion of data science and machine learning models in the decision-making process. This is because there is a need for decisions made by individuals and organizations when using these models to be accounted to someone or the other. It is particularly important where the autonomous systems of choices are made with no human supervision, such as in algorithmic decision-making in cases like those of autonomous cars and criminal justice systems. Who is responsible when the algorithm is wrong-for instance, mistakenly flagging someone with a high recidivism risk and giving that person a harsher sentence? Whose decision is it: the organization deploying the model, the data scientist who designed it, or the lawmakers sanctioning its deployment?

Data scientists need to have models that are interpretable: to answer that very question. That is, the reasoning chain of an algorithm leading to some decision ought to be intelligible and understandable to humans so that an interested party may scrutinize and interrogate those decisions. Explainability is particularly critical in high-stakes domains, such as medicine, where the difference can be literally a matter of life and death in regard to diagnosis or treatment. Here, the output of a black-box model becomes insufficient and needs to be supplemented with an explanation of how and why the model reached its conclusions so that health professionals and patients can make decisions.

It is not only the model's output but rather a whole process of data science-from collecting data to implementing models. Organizations need to come out clearly on what the people's data is being collected for and how it will be processed and for what purpose by making the public know about their practice of gathering and using their data. In addition to consent, this includes the ability to let individuals or people have choices to opt out of data collection anytime. Transparency will have to be the way in winning the trust of the public as they volunteer information more readily if they feel that they will not be mishandled and used wrongly.

Legal and regulatory frameworks too will have to be respected for ethical data science. Such strict laws will prevent businesses from simply collecting information on people and processing it the way they deem fit. Similar to how the EU has its General Data Protection Regulation, while in the US there is the California Consumer Privacy Act, it spits out several strict guidelines that govern collection and processing and sharing of data. All these laws need to be considered by the data scientists and their processes must look like compliance with all these laws. These policies consist of the observance of the data minimization practice which collects and stores only what serves its needs in providing help in their analysis and then the practice of anonymizing data that desensitizes the available dataset, removing personally identifiable information to keep private information protected.

Other than the data scientists making sure that it aligns with the law, ethical consideration of how it will affect society in general should be set by data science. Data science directly affects the outcomes of society since it is integrated into most decisions made within every industry. Therefore, data scientists creating those models have to be careful about probable uncontrolled outcomes that these models may lead to, especially in the fields of education, healthcare, and public policy. For example, a learning platform may contribute to socio-economic inequality, given that it would favor the students who are more likely to have increased access to computers as well as faster internet. Therefore, data scientists should really think about how they can build up their models to help alleviate social injustice and facilitate equal distribution of benefits from breakthroughs bred by data.

In a nutshell, ethical data science is integral to responsible practice rather than an ancillary concern. Data science continues transforming many industries and impacting the making of so many decisions. Therefore, data scientists, companies, and legislators should be putting ethical issues right at the top of their agenda: ensuring legal compliance, addressing bias and fairness, privacy and data security, and inspiring accountability and openness. With these ethical considerations, data scientists can use data in ways that bring positive social impact without violating the rights and dignity of people. Data science must cross complex ethical problems it generates with technological advances to ensure that all breakthroughs made possible by data gain significant utility for society at large.

# CHAPTER II

# The Data Science Process

## Knowledge of Data Science Workflow

Data science is the tool with which inferences valid from large datasets can be drawn to spur innovation and effective decision-making in diversely varied sectors. Data scientists follow a well-structured process widely referred to as a workflow to ensure that they handle data correctly and deliver insights relevant to the objectives of their projects. This is because the process of data science promises to offer effective and precise implementation of an activity, and hence, industry experts should be made aware of what the data science process contains. The workflow includes several steps, and every single step has its methods and strategies in place for the best possible solutions to problems. The section will focus on some of the major stages that the data science workflow has, which include collecting the data, cleaning data, exploratory data analysis, modeling, and interpretation.

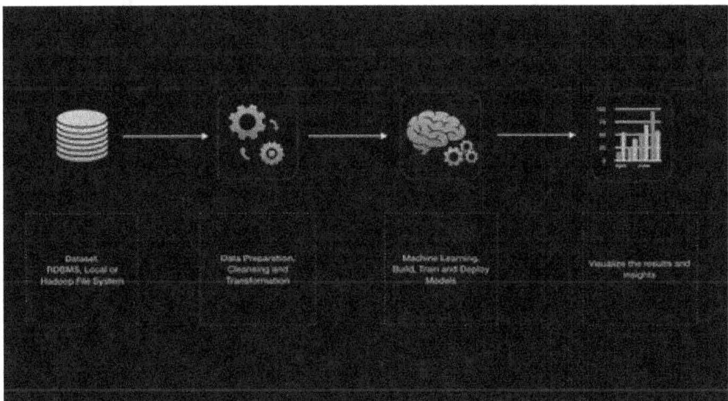


The data science pipeline initiates with data acquisition. This involves the collection of raw data from different sources. The quality and usability of collected data may significantly affect the conclusion of the analysis, and for that reason, this is one of the most crucial steps. Databases, sensors, web APIs, and social media are sources of data. Data scientists typically encounter structured as well as unstructured data. Data is structured if it is properly arranged in rows and columns of a database. However, techniques must involve more sophisticated processing forms to handle this kind of non-structured data, which will be text, photos, and videos. Sometimes, the process of collecting data integrates two different types of information into one data set. As such, for example, in a retail business, social media sentiment data may be aggregated with the transactional data of the customers in the point-of-sale system in order to generate a view of client behavior that is richer.

Data cleaning and preparation after the data is gathered, the subsequent processes occur in the pipeline. Since raw data is typically faulty, noisy, or incomplete, this is one of the key steps. Cleaning data removes all such anomalies and makes the data amenable to analytics. Raw data is likely to include outliers, duplications, or missing values. For instance, missing values might skew the findings of any analyses performed. For incomplete records, data scientists need to decide whether it makes sense to exclude them in their entirety or fill in missing values by interpolation-like methods. In case of findings of duplicate data, if not eliminated during preprocessing, then invalid conclusions may result, and even outliers can alter the results of some statistical models. This step involves further preprocessing-the process of putting data into a form one can utilize, such as scaling features to ensure that they lie within a similar range and normalizing numerical features or categorical variables. The step is intended to yield a clean, organized dataset that will be feasible for use in further investigation.

The second procedure of the data science workflow is exploratory data analysis, which eventually entails examining how the data behaves, how it will probably be distributed, and what one can anticipate when the data is analyzed. Data scientists engage in an extremely significant process called exploratory data analysis, EDA. Exploratory data analysis requires a data scientist to inspect the dataset in a way of gaining insight into the essentials of the dataset together with identifying the patterns, trends, and relationships. Data scientists use visualization and descriptive statistics in EDA to gain insights into the dataset. Some of the descriptive statistics data distribution might be summarized by mean, median, mode, variance, and standard deviation. Some of the applications of visualization tools include mainly histograms, scatter plots, and heatmaps, all of which are used in an effort to study how variables interact with each other and thereby subsequently reveal patterns buried in the data. A heatmap can express the strength of correlations among several variables, while a scatter plot is only able to suggest the existence of correlation of two variables with each other. The data scientists may follow an iterative process known as exploratory data analysis to unearth the hidden patterns in the data that could be helpful at a later stage while modeling.

Modeling phase, after EDA, makes predictions, classifies individual data observations, or points out the clusters using statistical and machine learning models applied to the data. Deciding which model to use will depend on what goals of the project are being addressed. For example, if somebody is looking to predict a continuous outcome such as sales revenue or temperature then regression models, for instance, linear regression or random forest regression, typically become the best utilized models. These algorithms are support vector machines, logistic regression, and decision trees amongst others, applicable to classify questions like that of spam/not spam email identity. Unsupervised learning is achieved through clustering methods, for example, k-means or hierarchical clustering, in customer segmentation, clumping together data points with common characteristics. In this sense, deeper models, like neural networks, can be used in deep learning, especially for the application in image identification and natural language processing.

Any model has to split data into two or more sets: the training set and the testing set. It is used in training of a model; the other is actually applied in the process of measuring how well the model performs over data that has not been tested. This step ensures that the model is not overfitting the training set and makes good generalization to new data. One that learns the noise or random fluctuations in the training set is an overfit model to the training set; this may lead to poor performance on new, untried data. Cross-validation, regularization, and pruning are some of the methods which may be used in prevention of overfitting. For cross-validation to ensure robustness, the data has to be divided into several subsets, and a model is trained on different combinations of these subsets. Two of the most widely used techniques to prevent over-complex models are L1 and L2 regularization. These avoid over-complex models by forcing the model to add a penalty term in the loss function; pruning is also a technique that removes branches from a decision tree that have a low predictive potential, thereby reducing the complexity of the tree.

Validation and interpretation is the subsequent stage of the workflow from the time the model is trained and tested. The most fundamental component of data science is the interpreting model, which ensures that the result and predictions are understandable and actionable for all stakeholders. Most the stakeholders need more information regarding technical details of a model, hence the need for effective as well as clear communication of findings by the data scientist. This can be as simple as explaining the coefficients and decisions made in a model in straightforward language or explaining how results from one model are sometimes conveyed through graphics. A data scientist may detail alterations to one variable, such as dollars marketed, that would affect the final, calculated predicted outcome like income from sales through a linear regression model. This step also needs to be validated as a subprocess to ensure that the domains of expertise and business goals match what the model is. To make derivations of this step useful for consideration in the problem at hand, correctness and reliability of the model are checked with validation.

After completing the training and testing of the model, it is important for data scientists to check how the model performs in terms of accuracy, precision, recall, F1 score, and area under the curve (AUC). The latter metrics provide a quantitative measure of the performance of the model on the test set. Other performance metrics such as MSE, MAE, and R-squared have been developed to estimate the predictive accuracy of regression models for continuous responses. In some of these situations, the data scientist needs to go back to earlier steps of the workflow, such as feature selection, cleaning, or algorithm tuning, to improve the model further. Most of the times, model tuning is about adjustment of hyperparameters, and every adjustment is done with a particular objective: improving performance. Optimized and validated, the model is ready for production.

A practical instance of deploying a model is when in integrating a model to a system or application to allow its use in the automation of decision-making processes or real-time predictions. For instance, an e-commerce website will implement a machine-learning-based recommendation system that offers particular product recommendations to customers based on specific needs. Similarly, a financial institution may deploy fraud-detection model within their transaction processing system to flag possible fraudulent activity. Data scientists and software engineers usually closely collaborate during the deployment phase to ensure the model is scalable, efficient, and reliable when deployed into the larger system. The deployment stage, on the other hand is not the last stage of the data science workflow. The model is constantly monitored and maintained to deliver performance over time. A model degrades mainly in dynamic environments characterized by time-varying trends and patterns when new fresh data crops up. It suffers from the problem of data drift, which is the process that brings about a shift in time in the statistical characteristics of the input data. Their models need periodically to be retrained and updated using fresh new data so as to remain accurate and relevant. Monitor the model execution in production with monitoring tools, which will readily spot early indicators of trouble, such as decreased accuracy or growing bias.

In a nutshell, the workflow of data science is a structured, iterative process that encompasses everything from data gathering to deployment and modeling. In each one of those workflow stages-data collection, cleaning, exploratory data analysis, modeling, interpretation, and validation-the accuracy, reliability, and utility of its insights are all critical. As a pre-requisite, data scientists need to understand the subtleties of the workflow in the solutions to difficult problems, wise judgments, and innovation in various sectors. This is still in the direction of a general structure that might lead to proper and effective analysis of data since data science is an emerging field.


## Formulating Issues and Goals

Defining a problem gives an opportunity to clearly define goals that produce successful outcomes in any field of study. Defining what needs to be targeted becomes the foundation of effective resource, time, and energy allocation between business, research, public policy, and personal development. In this section, it is described why the definition of the problems and goals is important, steps included, and how such well-defined goals affect decision making and solving.

The problem-solving process begins with identifying and stating the problems. The step of formulating an issue requires a grasp of the basic problems to be dealt with. An issue needs to know the situation more profoundly and the variables that affect the problem rather than outline what is wrong. It formulates both the symptoms and underlying causes of the issue. For example, in an organizational setting, just stating that sales went down may not capture the extent of the issue. Detailed analysis could discover factors such as changing preference by clients, growing competition or poor marketing strategies. Through this process, stakeholders can fine-tune their tactics based on circumstances peculiar to their situations with the proper definition of the issue at hand.

Typically, relevant information and discussion with the stakeholders form the base for formulating a problem. For pursuing information from different perspectives, it may involve conducting focus groups, questionnaires, and even interviews. For instance, hold a discussion with community folks, and you may obtain key information concerning the barriers that they face to get healthcare services in a project aimed to better public health. Apart from helping determine the problem, such data gathering and stakeholder participation promote a sense of ownership and cooperation from those affected by the situation. When stakeholders have a hand in formulating the issue, they are likely to feel more invested in possible solutions-a result more likely to be implemented.

Then comes the process of clearly defining the problems and setting objectives that derive solutions for such challenges. Objectives form guidelines for any venture, direct one's efforts, and concentrate them. They transform defined problems into goals to be achieved within a particular time-scale for their realization. You can engineer good goals applying SMART criteria on it: Specific, Measurable, Achievable, Relevant, and Time-bound. A measurable goal provides yardsticks for measuring success and progress, whereas a specific goal clearly articulates what needs to be done. Instead of having an open-ended objective like "sell more," a SMART goal could state something like "increase sales by 15% this quarter." Using the SMART criteria enables organizations and people to set crystal clear and achievable objectives that can be aligned with a greater mission.

Clear and relevant to the problems identified, goals should stand. Relevance of goals ascertains that work is being done on the right problems. Consider this: if the primary cause of less employee satisfaction proved is a lack of good interpersonal relationships among employees, then a goal concerning an increase in the number of team-building activities would be relevant in an organization seeking to enhance the level of satisfaction of its employees. However, focus on team-building alone cannot solve the root problem if low wages are the real problem that needs to be addressed. Therefore, it is important to evaluate repeatedly whether defined goals are really aligned with the issues they are supposed to solve. Periodic evaluations of the problem and the goals make possible the needed adjustments to the changed situation or new understanding made during the project. Formulation of problems and goals also involves iterative activities. New information may present new issues that require strategy shifts; hence, issues to be addressed and goals set need to be reassessed.

Adaptability is therefore very essential in a dynamic context where conditions may change within a quite short period-for example, changes in the demography of a population or emergence of a new disease within public health. If an organization identifies the mental health challenges are seriously impacting on communities' welfare, it can need to modify its initial aims to reduce obesity levels. The cyclical nature facilitates a never-stop learning process; thus, they are better at developing resilience if things do not go as planned.

The appropriately designed problems and objectives create an impact that is more than just a means of influencing behavior alone; instead, they are necessary for activating action at the individual and group levels. People are more likely to be interested and focused when they understand the issues that they are working on and can see how their efforts relate to the bigger picture of goals. Clearly defined goals generate a sense of purpose that fosters motivation and attention. While hazy or vague goals result in people getting lost and confused and, therefore, failing to understand where their efforts are being placed in the larger picture. In some organizations, employees often feel more satisfied with their job and become more productive.

Defining concerns and goals helps stakeholders to communicate and work together towards achievement, apart from motivating people inside an organization. Well-defined goals and problems give everyone who is part of the dialogue uniform terminology and framework, which makes teamwork easier. When everyone knows the issues and objectives, stakeholders might be in a better position to have more beneficial discourses and negotiations. This is particularly important in multidisciplinary situations where experts from several fields must work together to come up with complicated solutions. Particularly, scientists, politicians, and social personalities have to deliver the message of their comprehension in a clear manner, taking a synchronized approach toward designing comprehensive solutions to face climate change issues. Therefore, open communication and collaboration enable entities to utilize the collective experience of their stakeholder to achieve better quality outcomes.

Defining problems and goals is necessary for the assessment of progress and success. Having well set objectives gives performance a ready benchmark to work toward. Organizations through this are able to know what works and what needs a change as they monitor their progress toward the attainment of their objectives. If an organization choses its intention to reduce its carbon footprint by 20% in five years, it should track emission data on an annual basis to measure its progress. The stakeholders can collectively review the reasons and adjust their approach if it is clear that the company is failing to meet the objective. Apart from enhancing responsibility, this review mechanism develops a culture of continuous improvement because lessons learned become proper guides in projects.

Summarizing, defining problems and objectives are critical elements of making decisions as well as solving problems that fit any situation. A successful strategy starts with the identification and communication of the problems to be overcome, followed by meaningful and action-oriented objectives. The process requires information like relevant stakeholders, and the SMART criteria are applied to ensure that the objectives meet both specificity and measurement tests. The approach is also cyclical, permitting continuous learning while adapting to changing conditions. Well-conceived problems and objectives enable individuals and teams to eliminate obstacles and make a difference by motivating, developing teamwork, and allowing the evaluation. It is ultimately, then, the ability to set problems and objectives much more than a technical exercise; rather, they embody a core competency that drives innovation and productiveness across a range of industrial sectors and ensures that work is oriented to making a positive difference.

## Data Collection and Sourcing

Today, data-driven knowledge is absolutely necessary for organizations to make the right decisions. Data collection and acquisition are, therefore, integral parts of almost all business sectors, health care, social sciences, and environmental studies. The process of data collection allows an analysis of trends, patterns, and insights that spur innovative thinking and strategic efforts. However, the volume of data collected is not a measure of success for any data-driven strategy; it all depends on how relevant and of good quality that data is. This section examines the need to gather and source data and ways used, issues that arose, and the ethical issues to be considered.

The data collection process refers to the step-by-step generation of information for answering specific questions or fulfilling particular goals. It is a part of the research cycle through which businesses can transform disorganized data into a more intelligent form of knowledge. Data collection methods are very diverse, depending on study objectives, the type of data needed, and the resources available. More broadly, there are two general types of data-gathering techniques: quantitative and qualitative. The objective of quantitative data gathering is numerical data, and highly structured procedures, such as surveys, experiments, and observational studies, are often employed. The typical application of this kind of data is statistical methods used to discern patterns, relations, or causal relationships. On the other hand, collecting qualitative data aims to understand events on a deeper subjective level. This is ascertained through various methods such as focus group discussions, interviews, and ethnographic research, among many others. Researchers can gather data close to or reflective of the opinions, experiences, and motives of people. An appropriate method of collecting data is really a highly critical decision and should consist with the purposes of the inquiry.

For instance, a more advanced questionnaire with standardized questions will give a more 'certain' quantifiable outcome if it aims to find out the satisfaction of customers at different levels regarding a new product. On the other hand, open-ended questions in the survey or interviews offer much context if they aims at knowing the customers' thinking and ideas behind the product. In this regard, entities can assess the objectives and the kind of data needed to generate smart decisions on the most appropriate methods for their data collection activities. Data searching on the other hand, is defined as the process of finding and collecting the data needed for analysis.

This technique includes sources of data that include a primary source and a secondary source. Primary data refers to information that is collected directly for a specified purpose of a study. This can be achieved through surveys, experiments, interviews, and even direct first-hand observations. The main advantage is that primary data is specific and relevant because it directly addresses topics under study. However, collecting primary data takes lots of time and effort, especially to gather large samples. Secondary data is the existing data available today. It can be found through current sources such as databases, scholarly journals, internet archives, and official documents. Using secondary data, particularly, is economical and resource-friendly, very much when time is at a limit. Big data revolutionized the sourcing of data to enable utilization of humongous volumes of information produced by multiple avenues, such as social media, online commerce, and Internet of Things devices.

It could conceivably identify important knowledge on consumer behavior, industry trends, or operational efficiency from such a source. But such large and varied types of data also pose great challenges. Of course, an organization needs to have robust methods of ascertaining sources of reliable information for the purpose of filtering noise data that could be more relevant and reliable. Furthermore, because big data is dynamic, businesses must constantly alter their sourcing plans to maintain the pace with a data environment in constant change. Despite these aggregating and sourcing benefits, there are several issues that will be encountered down the track:. Ensuring data quality is a very big problem. Quality data consists of characteristics such as accuracy, consistency, correctness, and completeness—poor quality in data results in financial losses, wrong conclusions, and inappropriate initiatives. Helping the problem of data quality issues would be achieved if organizations formulate a framework of data governance, implement validation procedures for data, and fund staff training on best practice about collecting data. Other quality control measures that would help bring out inconsistencies are frequency audits of data sources and procedures. Other challenges in the gathering and sourcing process include safeguarding information about data safety and confidentiality issues.

With the widespread Ness of gathering data practices, it has become very essential to protect the right of privacy for individuals. Organizations need to adhere to many laws, like CCPA and GDPR, which are very strict in terms of collection, storage, and processing of personal data. If it fails to do so, the organization's will be heavily penalized and their reputation will be hampered. In dealing with such a problem, organizations must apply ethical methods of collection, obtain informed consent from the respondents, and ensure that the outcome on how the data is going to be used is well defined. Apart from privacy concerns, there are chances that organizations encounter biases in terms of collecting and sourcing data. Sources of bias generally fall into the following categories: Words used in a question during the surveying.

Environment where data is being collected. For instance, information of a particular survey that mainly targets only one classification of people may be distorted because it lacks opinion from the population. Social media may also give only information based on the views of frequent users, therefore may omit the opinions of another silent and vital aspect in society. On the other hand, the process of gathering data can be reduced to its lowest minimum by adopting many strategies and trying to draw a representative sample. Moreover, sources of the data utilized should be critically appraised by the researchers. Obviously, no one may dispute the fact that technology plays a very important role in data discovery and gathering.

It is now easier for organizations to collect and analyze data much faster than before due to the huge process streamlining that is available currently concerning advance in data collection tools, such as mobile applications, online sites for surveying, as well as software tools associated with data analytics. Moreover, as machine learning and artificial intelligence are increasingly used in the automation of gathering and processing data, organizations will find it easy to create timely insight followed by decision implementation. Such companies can tap into web scraping technologies, among others, to gain data from websites and then carry on analyzing the extracted information to identify trends in the market. Technology can be utilized to improve upon the gathering of the data, and in so doing, it also carries out the risks of such developments being exemplified, the very real dangers of perils from data breaches and ethical dilemmas from the inclusion of automated systems. Organizations require great importance to be given to effective methods of data gathering and sourcing as the importance of making a decision with data is increasing every single day.

This requires the process of trustworthy data sourcing procedures, proper selection of methods, and a deep understanding of the objectives for data compilation. Exploiting both primary and secondary sources of data will enable organizations to have extensive information that may elicit ingenuity and effectiveness. Attention to privacy issues and ethical concerns, including the quality of data, is what will make credibility and reliability precede all other stakeholders. Data gathering and curating form part of what help make any data-based project work. Systematic information gathering alongside the discovery of sources that one can rely on affords businesses great riches in terms of information which acts to inform strategic decisions and operationality.

While the process has been subject to many challenges, including quality in data, and privacy concerns, and limitations that create biases. Such organizations can effectively manage those obstacles coming their way from the very start to obtain the benefits by a proper amalgamation of the techniques involved in information technology, ethical principles, and stakeholder engagements in the collection of data. By doing this, it will establish a powerful ecosystem for the safeguarding of smart choices, and resultant good results in every day to day life because as it is nowadays becoming increasingly complicated and dynamic. In the future, therefore, the importance of effective data gathering and acquisition will be only higher because data is very precious even to this day.

## Data Cleaning and Preparation

Data preparation and cleaning is a function that is nearly impossible to replace in data science. Organizations will only be able to base decisions more and more on data if they use good-quality data. It involves finding errors and inconsistencies in a database and correcting them. This process ensures that the gathered data is accurate, complete, and analytically useful. Data preparation, however, encompasses all the more general tasks involved in processing raw data into a form of analysis. These procedures work in synergy to have a conditioning effect of a high degree on the nature of the findings from analysis and what one will be able to derive from the data. They are, therefore, highly important tasks in completing any data analysis exercise.

Clean the data in this case, the cleaning of data refers to knowing the kind and the structure. This means passing through the dataset to find possible problems, outliers, inconsistencies, and missing numbers. Missing data is one of the common problems with datasets that may result from many sources, such as problems of data integration or malfunction or human error of equipment. Missing data may lead to some form of bias in the output of some analysis and give wrong conclusions; it is thus necessary to handle missing data. Some ways of handling missing data include interpolation, imputation, or deletion, among others. Deletion might be appropriate, for instance, if there are very few missing values, and deletion is removing records that have some missing values. However, this method may lose important data if a higher number of records are deleted. However, replacement means filling or imputing the missing numbers by statistical techniques or algorithms. In this method, mean replacement is one of them; here, it replaces the missing numbers by the average of available data. Imputation can assist in keeping your data valid but do not render the dataset biased on account of the imputation step.

Outliers are those data points that have far deviated from other observations of the dataset. The reason for outliers can be the consequence of faults in measurements, faulty inputting of data, or simply variability in data. The outliers usually have a dramatic influence on the outcome of the statistical analysis or model, so they must be found and corrected. Some of them must change or be marked for future analysis. Other methods, such as z-scores and the IQR method, can be utilized to locate outliers in the data set by determining how far a data point is from either the mean or median. While it may be a very strong urge to drop outliers without further examination, there is a need to know how they arose, if they are indeed errors or legitimate variation that deserves to be included.

Failure to show values or variability of the data can also bar analysis and, in effect, outliers. It may arise where the data sources are several and then deliver different naming conventions, coding schemes, or formats. For instance, the same class can be represented in the same set with a number of appearances, for example, "NY," "New York," and "New York City," as referring to the same place. This inconsistency would be prone to misrepresenting it, making analysis challenging, and consequently, leads to wrong interpretations. Thus, standardization is needed to address such discrepancies. It can define a standard format for data and may standardize categories, transform all text to lower case, and use uniform date formats. In many ways, data standardization improves data quality and analytical efficiency and facilitates a comparison and aggregation of data from many sources.

Making cleaned data-analytical form is data preparation, which means putting cleaned data into an analytical format; because, for instance, frequently scaling or normalizing data is sometimes necessary when algorithms are sensitive to the variety of input features. In case of some techniques that do algorithmic machine learning such as k-means clustering and support vector machines, the scale of the data can really make a difference. Standardization transforms all data so that it has a mean of 0 and the standard deviation is equal to 1, whereas normalization usually refers to rescaling your data such that they fall within some certain range- probably [0, 1]. This transformation works towards the fact that only some characteristics of the data would tend to overpower the analysis because of their size. One other sub-tasks in preprocessing the data is feature engineering. Feature engineering is the process by which relevant variables are selected, transformed, and sometimes even generated with a view towards improving a model's ability to make predictions in general. New variables can be defined from existing ones through feature engineering. For example, unit price and quantity sold might be put together to create the variable "total sales." Other types of categorical data-to-numerical translations may also be required so that algorithms can better grasp what such variables signify. Proper feature engineering is necessary to enhance the effectiveness of the machine learning models and generally impacts the results that are going to be derived from the research.

It's very important to document the whole process of data preparation and cleaning properly. Thus, clear documentation provides transparency but also ensures that the steps taken can be replicated or understood by others who might eventually work with the data later on. That is very important in teams where an individual can have many members working together who can analyze datasets collectively. Documentation should also include the processes applied during cleaning and preparation, changes made, and the justification of the choices. That way, transparency can encourage more informed discussions about ramifications from their conclusions. In addition, confidence in the outcomes of the analysis will be nurtured. Although most of the advantages of cleaning and preparing data occur at this stage, sometimes the processes encounter challenges. One of these challenges, particularly in the era of big data, is that enterprises could be dealing with humongous volumes of data. There are times when large data sets command too much of the resources and require special management as well as tools to handle them. For example, distributed processing frameworks like Apache Spark can facilitate big dataset handling by distributing the workloads between various nodes. With such technologies, businesses can gain better insights through streamlined preparation of data and cleaning of data.

The second problem is that of source complexity in modern data. Data come from numerous sources: text documents, spreadsheets, databases, social media, unstructured, and even semi-structured sources. Various sources have to be brought into cohesion and must employ complex techniques of data integration so that a cohesive dataset can be had for further analysis. This process can be entirely mechanized through the use of ETL systems, which extract data from multiple sources, standardize the formats and load it into one repository for analysis. From the technical standpoint, an organization has to address the ethical concerns of data preparation and cleaning. In the right environment, and if outlier removing or missing value imputing is implemented correctly, then unnoticed bias also might creep into the data. This could be the case because, for instance, those imputation techniques that do not account for the fact that some groups are systematically underrepresented in the data might delay some inequities found in the final analysis. This implies that ethical considerations must therefore play a critical role in the stage of data preparation and cleaning so that the analysis is fair and just.

Data preparation and cleaning form part of the different stages in the analytics process, whereby they are so necessary that they influence the dependability and quality of the findings from the data directly. Organizations would then improve the accuracy and reliability of their datasets by finding and correcting errors, inconsistencies, and missing values. Good data preparation also ensures that data can be applied for well-informed decisions because it prepares it for meaningful analysis through feature engineering, scaling, and normalization. Data preparation and cleaning remain relevant today, but they can now be scaled more easily for big data as well as integrate heterogeneous sources of data and address questions of ethicality. Establishing such foundational processes as a number one priority can help firms really exploit their data as they navigate the vagaries of an increasingly data-driven world, generating better outcomes and competitive advantage.

## Exploratory Data Analysis

Realignment into a much more formal statistical modeling framework can thus be well dealt with the help of exploratory data analysis, that is, an integral part of the cycle of data analysis in which researchers and analysts come to have a better feel for what is going on in their data. EDA was first formulated by statistician John Tukey in the 1970s, emphasizing the use of visual supports together with elementary statistics so that the evidence can be examined without even assuming it or making conjectures. Now, EDAs, therefore, discover facets of the data; hence, the right decisions are made, and further probing is led. This section outlines the purposes, procedures, and importance of exploratory data analysis within the context of modern data science.

EDA aims to identify hidden structures or relationships and to summarize a collection of information through its most salient features. Preliminary exploration is essential for further development and provides grounds for scientists to formulate theories and select appropriate modeling strategies. Data cleaning and preparation is the first step of EDA that ensures data becomes properly formatted for investigation. During this phase, missing values, outliers, and inconsistencies are dealt with because they significantly impact outcomes from analysis. For instance, outliers pull distributions in skewed ways, and missing values may result in misleading statistical estimates. Data analysts give a clean dataset that is bound to offer a confirmed ground for the exploration of solving these issues.

Data analysis could mark the beginning of the exploratory stage following data cleaning and transformation. Visualizations are some of the best tools used during data exploration. Graphical representations are the most important tools in EDA since they provide immediate insights into distributions, trends, and patterns of data. Some of the most frequently used visualization methods include heatmaps, box plots, scatter plots, and histograms-for a particular purpose. Histograms are applied in representing regions of concentration and possible skewness in the distribution of one variable. Box plots will facilitate gathering data for easy visualization such that quartiles and outliers can easily be pointed out through the overall spread and central tendency of data. Scatter plots are pretty useful for detecting potential clusters and the relationship between two quantitative variables. Heatmaps can be used to exhibit complex relationships with the aim of highlighting values along two dimensions instead of intensity.

In addition to visualization, an extremely important tool applied in EDA is descriptive statistics. Analysts can compute to meaningfully understand central tendency and dispersion of data by metrics such as the mean, median, mode, standard deviation, and variance. These figures allow for a numerical summary of the dataset which can sustain an overview of important features, like general trends and variability. For instance, skewness of a sample would be approximated comparing the mean value and median value that were computed for the sample, so the standard deviation would depict to the analyst the degree by which the data were dispersed from the mean. Descriptive statistics makes such quantitative context meaningful for visualizations.

Finding associations of variables is another part of exploratory data analysis and is important. This is particularly important when working with multivariate datasets since many different factors could be in play when it comes to the outcome. Analysts very often use correlation coefficients to estimate the direction and strength of correlations between sets of continuous variables. The correlation coefficient is just the number between -1 and +1 that captures how much two variables move together. Coefficients close to +1 are strong positive correlations, whereas coefficients close to -1 indicate strong negative correlations. To interpret these, analysts might discover some predictors or confounding variables that could affect the analysis.

EDA can also be helpful in checking the assumptions underlying some of the statistical methods. Some tests assume specific types of data, e.g. linear regression: the observations are independent, homoscedastic, and normally distributed. Analysts can apply EDA to check those kinds of assumptions visually on data, which will help them determine whether they need some more classical modeling methods. For instance, if one wishes to check whether a given dataset is normally distributed, then the quantiles of data can be compared with the quantiles of a normal distribution for such a purpose by using a Q-Q plot. If observations fall close to the line of reference, the data will be considered approximately regularly distributed. Otherwise, analysts have to consider some other techniques' application or transforming in some way for mitigating violated assumptions.

Although data exploration is the most critical one, what matters more is EDA as it goes hand in hand with communication and storytelling. In fact, the ability to clearly communicate story-Drive by data-driven findings will be crucial in this new age of data-driven decision-making. EDA has made it easier to interpret complex data streams as narratives that can easily be understood by a decision-maker in as few facts as possible. Graphical presentations and summary statistics are helpful to illustrate trends, relationships, and deviations in a manner that can be easily understood even for non-technical audiences; hence it fosters teamwork and develops a data-driven organizational culture, whereby decision making can be based on evidence.

Exploratory data analysis is disadvantageous despite the various advantages. The most important limitation of EDA is that it only ever produces an interpretation of the data if performing formal hypothesis testing. Such decisions cannot be made with trends and intuition derived from EDA. Analysts should, using their discretion, interpret the findings of EDA regarding confounding factors or biases that might have crept in while conducting it. Overdependence on visualizations may also result in misinterpretation, say bad design or worse still, with malicious intent to deceive the users. This is, however, a reason why EDA, despite being an extremely efficient tool for exploratory data analysis can only be used with exhaustive statistical analysis and hypothesis testing to arrive at valid results. Another criticism related to EDA is the danger of information overload. Living in an era of abundance where data is abundant, analysts need more information. It tends to obscure basic patterns or insights in noise and complexity. Analysts need to approach EDA in a structured manner with specific objectives and questions in order to avoid this problem. Therefore, focusing on the study of the relevant factors and their correlation might make it easier and less time-consuming to come up with a clearer insight.

Exploratory data analysis has completely changed the modern landscape of technology. The latest developments in programming languages and data visualization tools have made EDA much more efficient and accessible. The analysts can run deep studies and make interactive visuals through Tableau, Power BI, and Python modules like Matplotlib and Seaborn. Most importantly, at present, EDA techniques need to be new enough to meet the very big and complex data volumes that exist within the database of modern data sources, keeping in view an increasing flow of huge data and machine learning. Such techniques as clustering and dimensionality reduction allow analysts to uncover what is hidden in high-dimensional data.

Exploratory data analysis, in short words, is an integral part of the analysis process since it allows analysts and researchers with tools and methodology for "exploring" their data in the pursuit of understanding. EDA simplifies the revealing of patterns, correlations, or outliers through descriptive statistics and visualizations that make it easier to provide well-informed decisions and hypotheses that have been produced. An area of statistics like this can be analyzed for hidden assumptions that lie in place, thus allowing analysts to warrant the foundation that their findings stand on truly. In addition to providing a basis for how companies can create a culture of data and collaboration, EDA is critical in the sharing of insight. As outlined above, there are several areas for improvement to using EDA. Nevertheless, EDA is considered a vital tool for today's data scientist. The future of the evolution of data analysis will ultimately decide precisely how analysis is conducted as more data becomes widely available.

# CHAPTER III

# Machine Learning Fundamentals

## Introduction to Machine Learning

Machine learning is part of AI probably the most disruptive technology this century. Thanks to statistical methods and algorithms, computers can predict and even decide things based on data. Unlike ordinary programming, in which you have to feed the computer step-by-step instructions, machine learning allows systems to learn and automatically improve in the process. This section discusses the basic concepts of machine learning, its types, applications, problems, and possible future trends.

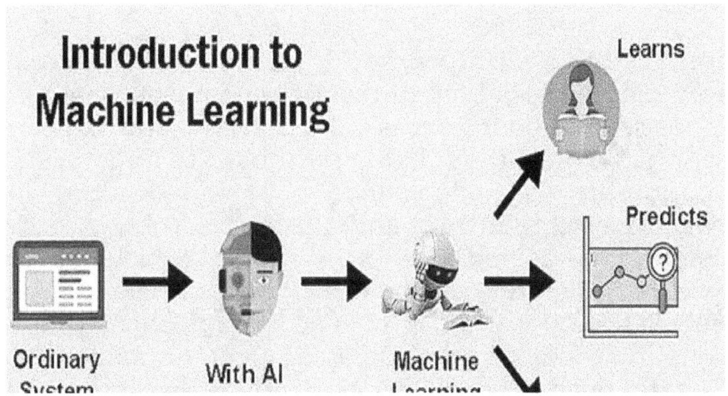


The general concept most associated with the term machine learning is the use of data to train models. A definition of machine learning model is a type of algorithm that accepts inputting new data for analysis to discover patterns and make some suggestions or predictions. With more data fed into it to train on, the more it generalizes its predictions on unseen examples. For instance, based on the patterns that the training set would have learned, a model that was trained on a data set of text e-mails may classify the emails as "spam" or "not spam." The better the diversified and the bigger the training data is, the better the performance the model is likely to do.

The three significant types that machine learning may be roughly classified into are supervised learning, unsupervised learning, and reinforcement learning. This is actually the practice of training a model on a dataset with labeled inputs and desired outputs provided. A lot of times, this is applied to jobs such as regression and classification. Classifying tasks, for example, whether an incoming email is spam or not, will teach the model to categorize incoming data into predefined classes. In regression problems, the model predicts continuous data, for example, house price against location and size. The other common algorithms include support vector machines and then decision trees, and finally the linear regression.

Contrastingly, unsupervised learning is actually developing a model on an unlabeled dataset where it is supposed to identify the relationships and patterns existing in data without being prompted to do that. Such an approach is quite effective for applications like dimensionality reduction and clustering. The process of clustering is carried out by a model, which merges similar data points based on their intrinsic characteristics. In fact, if a shop wanted to take advantage of customized marketing techniques, it could use clustering algorithms to categorize its population of customers into subsections on the basis of their purchase behavior. Amongst these techniques is principal component analysis, which is a technique in data reduction; thus, it will reduce the complexity of data by reducing the number of features in a manner important to information. This will be very useful in problems that will have high-dimensional data which will lead to issues with visualization and inefficiency.

Another type of machine learning is reinforcement learning whose emphasis is on the training of agents on how to behave so that there is maximization of cumulative rewards. This approach allows the agent to learn through trial and error using rewards or punishments for action taken. Compared to reinforcement learning, applications in various successful fields by developing autonomous systems, robotics, and games are such crucial examples. For instance, DeepMind's AlphaGo effectively proved the power of reinforcement learning when they went past the world champions in Go, one of the most challenging board games in history. After tens of thousands of self-play and simulations, the AI finally learned the best tactics that surpass human capacity.

Machine learning is now being applied by various sectors and industrial domains. Now, it has revolutionized how business actually works and makes decisions, in addition to streamlining each aspect of an organization. In healthcare, for example, the machine learning algorithms assess patient data on disease outcomes and aids in the diagnosis process and in developing customized treatment programs. The predictive models could determine those who are highly prone to specific diseases and possible early treatments or preventive measures. Machine learning can be applied to algorithmic trading in the financial world, credit scoring, and fraud detection. This has several advantages: As a financial institution analyzes trends in transactions, they can determine losses due to fraudulent activity and identify anomalies.

The retail industry has also used machine learning to enhance customer care, handle stock while improving sales. Recommendation systems apply the machine learning algorithms in rating consumer behavior and preferences then contribute appropriate products for consumers to buy. These promote high sales and conversion rates besides improved customer satisfaction.

It also applies machine learning in demand prediction and coordination of logistics and overhead reduction making supply chains more responsive and efficient. Generally, machine learning is widely applied in traditionally dominated areas as well as very significantly impacts the new domains such as self-driving vehicles, smart cities among others. Machine learning algorithms process large volumes of sensor data thus allowing the self-driving cars to identify objects and navigate through challenging environments through decision making in an instance. This addition of machine learning in smart city initiatives improves on resource utilization, traffic management, and physical urban design hence improving the quality of living by its residents.

Machine learning has many advantages and applications but also some problems that need to be solved in order to be applied efficiently. The first major obstacle is the need for quality data. The proper performance of machine learning models depends on the quality and quantity of training data. In many cases, there is a limitation in obtaining enough labeled data; for instance, this is due to an area of application needing to be narrow and specialized, like medicine or incident, hardly occurring. Furthermore, noisy, skewed, and missing data could cause improper performance of a model and have serious ethical implications. These require to be dealt with through very robust data preparation techniques and data integrity.

Interpretability is one of the biggest challenges in machine learning. It's generally very hard to know how many machine learning models, especially complicated ones like deep neural networks, achieve results because they tend to operate as "black boxes." This is especially problematic in high-stakes applications such as healthcare or finance, where it is important to know not only what is being done but also why. Research is underway in making the models more interpretable so that better feels are provided to stakeholders on what the algorithm is actually deciding upon. The development and use of machine learning systems also critically depend on ethical issues. Systemic consequences can arise from inappropriate or biased data. For example, unless the algorithm in predictive policing algorithms is trained on prior crime data that reflects such biases, systemic prejudices would again be perpetuated in future enforcement tactics. Thus, it would be desirable to build up ethical frameworks and rules that ensure equity, accountability, and transparency in its implementations as machine learning advances.

It will surely remain huge for innovation and growth when it is considered as machine learning into the future. With better processing power and more available data, the models would be only growing more complex. A particularly exciting subset of machine learning is deep learning, where attention is given to multi-layered neural networks; already such a tool has succeeded in creating powerful speech recognition, natural language processing capabilities, and many other feats of image recognition. The architectures and methods will come out new, so certainly, machine learning is going to be more versatile and applicable in solving more problems. Some of the other emerging technologies that will further help advance machine learning capabilities include edge computing and the Internet of Things (IoT). The IoT devices themselves generate huge data volumes. Real-time algorithms of machine learning can tap insights from these data volumes to simplify the process. For instance, smart home appliances may well detect user preferences and even auto-update energy usage, making all processes involving it easier and more efficient. It really benefits applications that are of real-time liking, such as self-driven cars and industrial automation, due to the handling process of processing more data closer to its originating source with a real effect on speed for decisions and latency reduction.

Put, machine learning is a paradigm shift in the way we interact with data and how it is used to make predictions and judgment. It has been a driving force of innovation across industries and transformed several sectors by opening windows to the possibility of computers learning from data and hence improving over time. It becomes such a strong tool in today's data-driven world to reveal the patterns that weren't known and also streamline processes that will enhance the user experience. However, issues of data quality, interpretability, and ethics will make responsible development and implementation of machine learning systems necessary. As the technology develops and the appetite for intelligent solutions grows, machine learning will certainly be one of the key determining factors in the progression of our society.

## Supervised Learning Techniques

A basic area of supervised learning is where the algorithms are trained on labeled datasets in order to generate predictions or judgments. This is attained through minimizing the discrepancy between its predicted and actual values, thus enabling the proper mapping of inputs to their corresponding outputs. The approach is based on input-output pairings. Supervised learning is one of the skills a data scientist should have in his toolbox because this approach has been massively used in domains such as picture identification and email filtering. This section is a thorough review of this very important domain in machine learning, exploring the major supervised learning approaches, including applications, benefits, and limitations.

The most widespread application of supervised learning is linear regression as applied to predicting continuous outcomes. In this regard, linear regression utilizes a linear equation that has an expression of a relationship between an input and output variable. The technique thus aims to find the line with the best fit by the data points where the summation of the squared discrepancies between the anticipated and actual values is minimized. Because linear regression is user-friendly and easier to interpret, it is often used for scenarios where it is expected that a linear relationship exists between the variables. With complicated relationships or multicollinearity of input features, however, its performance needs to improve.

Another quite commonly applied technique of the family of supervised learning algorithms, logistic regression, is particularly apt for classification problems with only two classes of solutions. Unlike linear regression, logistic regression makes use of the logistic function to predict how likely it is for that particular input to fall into a given class. This function works well in situations where the result is categorical since it converts any input to a value between 0 and 1. Given its efficiency and readability, logistic regression is preferred, especially when there is a roughly linear relationship between independent factors and the log-odds of the dependent variable. The principal drawback of logistic regression involves an assumption about the independence of the independent variables against the log-odds relationship with the result, which may be different in many real applications.

Another very powerful and effective supervised learning approach is a decision tree, which can be applied to both regression and classification tasks. The algorithm divides the dataset into subsets iteratively based on values of input features and thus forms a model like that of a tree. Each leaf node represents the output value, each branch represents a decision rule, and each internal node represents a feature. Decision trees are popular with practitioners because they are easy to use and intuitive. They are also insensitive to scale and can be utilized for categorical as well as numerical data. Decision trees are prone to overfitting in case it is allowed to grow too deep. This problem may be removed using techniques like pruning, boosting methods or ensemble methods like Random Forests.

Random Forests is an ensemble method where several decision trees work together for a more comprehensive and accurate model than produced by a single decision tree algorithm, a technique that improves upon the algorithm of decision trees. To introduce variety to the model, each tree is trained using a different random subset of the characteristics and data. The last prediction is achieved by averaging all the predictions made by each individual tree, normally through averaging for regression tasks and voting for classification problems. In comparison with the single decision tree, it decreases the tendency of overfitting and enables the model to have greater generalization capacity. Because Random Forest is able to discover the most significant features and interactions, this method is particularly valuable in very large high-dimensional data sets. However, compared with other more simple models, their interpretability may be more challenging.

Another widely applied method of supervised learning is that of support vector machines. This is particularly well-known for the ability in high-dimensional spaces. By the application of SVM, one determines which is the best hyperplane which separates points of different classes. The maximum margin that could be obtained between data points belonging to each class-nearest to the hyperplane and therefore termed as support vectors- is maximized. In fact, utilizing the kernel functions operation, SVM also allows one to tackle nonlinear decision boundaries by reducing the input space into a higher dimension in which a linear separation becomes possible. Thus, due to its adaptability, SVM is an extremely effective tool for classification jobs, especially when facing conditions involving complicated decision boundaries. However, a careful selection of a suitable kernel along with tuning the hyperparameters may pose difficult issues, and SVM can be computationally expensive, especially when dealing with really huge datasets.

The other type of supervised learning method is neural networks. They are best suited for very challenging tasks such as speech recognition, image recognition, and natural language processing. Artificial neurons in the network are arranged into multiple layers, and each one processes inputs to output its result to the layer above. The network learns through the optimization algorithms, such as gradient descent, by adjusting its weight according to errors between predictions and actual values. Neural networks are computationally intensive, thus capable of scaling up to large complex data sets. While they do exceptionally well at spotting very small data-internal patterns, they are often much harder to interpret than other supervised learning methods because of their complexity, and they do require lots and lots of data and powerful computers to work at their best.

Deep learning is one of the recent concepts of supervised learning and is the subfield of the neural network that engages with several hidden layers. Two of the examples of the deep learning model are CNNs and RNNs. Both of them have shown very impressive results in a wide range of applications. CNNs are very good at image processing application mainly due to their ability to automatically get features and spatial hierarchies from images. RNNs are most frequently applied to time series prediction and natural language processing tasks because they are specifically designed for the sequential data. Deep learning methods have shown great promise across many sectors for handling unstructured data and achieving state-of-the-art performance in several areas. However, the chief disadvantages are a few significant ones: the basic requirement for large datasets of labeled examples and the possibility of overfitting.

There are a number of different supervised learning methods, and they share a few common ills. Among the worst of these is overfitting: a model, which performs extremely well on training data, yet needs to generalize to fresh, untried data. In other words, overfitting happens when the model identifies noise in the training data rather than identifying some real underlying pattern. Techniques like regularization, cross-validation, and model simplification are typically applied by practitioners to avoid overfitting. Cross-validation breaks the data set into several subsets and, therefore, tends to estimate how well the model should generalize better to data that was not observed. L1 and L2 are two regularization strategies that penalize complex models and, therefore, push solutions that generalize more broadly.

Another challenge in supervised learning relates to the quality and quantity of available labeled data. In most real-world applications, it is cumbersome and resource-intensive to obtain a dataset of appropriate size with labels. Moreover, suboptimal performance of the model can be caused by incorrect labeling of data, so the quality of labels becomes very important. Tow two answers to this problem are semi-supervised learning and active learning. Semi-supervised learning increases learning accuracy by mixing a little amount of labeled input with a much larger amount of unlabeled data. Contrast to this, active learning goes by iteratively querying a human expert or oracle to classify the most informative data points thereby learning much more with far fewer labeled data.

Another challenge remains in the interpretability of supervised learning models, especially when using more sophisticated methods such as deep learning. It is harder and harder to understand exactly how the models actually arrive at specific predictions as its complexity increases. Such a lack of interpretability is worrying, especially for high-stakes domains such as healthcare and finance in which stakeholders have to be able to trust and understand how the model made its decisions. Researchers are actively working on improving interpretability techniques such as SHAP (SHapley Additive exPlanations) and LIME (Local Interpretable Model-Agnostic Explanations) to better expose the contributions of specific features towards the predictions of the model. Yet despite these challenges, supervised learning remains one of the basic elements of machine learning, driving advancement in hundreds of areas and industries. Since supervised learning methods can easily be adapted, practitioners can use the benefits of several algorithms to tailor their strategies to specific tasks and data sets. Supervised learning solutions are highly in demand because more and more firms have realized that deciding with data is not only crucial but also the only way forward.

This indicates a bright future for the field of supervised learning because studies are being done with the aim of enhancing the effectiveness and precision and clarity of these techniques. An AutoML solution is supposed to ease access to supervised learning for nontechnical personnel because it streamlines the process of selecting and fine-tuning algorithms. Furthermore, breakthroughs in transfer learning-the process of taking advantage of information gained from one task in order to improve performance on a related task-reopen the vista of expanding the domains to which supervised learning techniques can be generalized.

To recap, supervised learning techniques constitute the backbone of machine learning theory because they provide powerful tools for prediction and selection among classified examples. These methods vary from as complex as a neural network to a simple linear regression, and there are an array of solutions for addressing a huge range of problems. While issues persist with overfitting, data quality, and interpretability, further study and development in this field slowly open doors to more reliable, efficient supervised learning techniques. Supervised learning, of course, is going to be part of the future of machine learning as it entails new technology, thus defining the future of data-driven decision-making in so many different industries.

## Unsupervised Learning Techniques

The most basic type of machine learning is unsupervised learning, training algorithms from data without labeled results. Unsupervised learning focuses on finding underlying patterns or intrinsic structures within the data; supervised learning, on the other hand, trains models to map input data to specific outputs depending on labels supplied. The method is very helpful when seeking goals such as the exploration of data, finding groups or clusters, and reducing dimensionality since it can unfurl insights that lead to better decision-making. This section presents a detailed review of this important field of machine learning by looking at some unsupervised learning strategy, their applications, advantages, and disadvantages.

Clustering is a wide unsupervised learning algorithm that groups similar data points along a set of specific attributes. The most widely used algorithm in clustering algorithms today is K-means, which partitions the data into K separate subsets. First, centroids are initialized arbitrarily to K. Then, each data point is assigned repeatedly to the closest centroid using some notion of distance, such as Euclidean distance. After all the points are transferred, the centroids are updated by averaging all the points inside each of the clusters. This process continues until the centroids no longer change noticeably.

Because of the simplicity of its application and flexibility, K-means is preferred for handling big datasets. However, the performance completely depends upon the initial centrocentric positioning and a choice of K that often needs to be clarified. Furthermore, K-means assumes that clusters have roughly equivalent sizes and spherical shapes, which may lead to more than optimal solutions when dealing with complex data distributions.

Hierarchical clustering is a second very powerful unsupervised learning technique. While K-means requires a-priori specification of the number of groups, hierarchical clustering performs the entire job at one go, depicting the interrelationships between points through a dendrogram or a tree structure. Two widely used approaches to splitting the algorithm are agglomerative and divisive. Agglomerative clustering starts at each data point in a separate cluster and iteratively combines the closest pairings of clusters until one cluster is left or a specified number is attained. Divisive clustering starts with one cluster and repeatedly splits it into smaller clusters. Hierarchical clustering gives a more detailed view of the structure by cutting the dendrogram at several heights, thereby allowing the practitioner to study several levels of granularity. This approach is however sensitive to noise and outliers, and computationally heavy, particularly for high dimensional data.

Another important unsupervised learning technique is dimensionality reduction, or put, lowering the number of features or variables in a dataset whilst preserving its intrinsic structure. This helps to mitigate the dimensionality curse and improves the effectiveness of other machine learning algorithms, making it particularly suited to high-dimensional data. Among the principal ways of reducing dimensionality are PCA-Principal Component Analysis. PCA works to identify the primary directions, or components, through which data fluctuates most. While compressing the dimensionality, PCA retains the largest amount of variability by projecting the data onto these components. It also helps find hidden patterns in complex datasets and, therefore, depicts them easily. However, PCA may not work very well on the datasets with nonlinear structures as it assumes a linear relation between features.

The second dimensionality reduction algorithm most popular for its effectiveness in visualizing high-dimensional data is known as t-Distributed Stochastic Neighbor Embedding. t-SNE focuses more on preserving local structures of data than does PCA, which seeks to maximize variance. Similarity between the data points is converted into probabilities and minimized as far as divergence of such probabilities from the original to reduced dimensions is concerned. It can create two- or three-dimensional representations of data focusing on patterns and clusters. The t-SNE's powerful ability to visualize complex datasets makes it of great utility; this is quite common in image processing and genomics contexts. Computational intensity and strong reliance on hyperparameter selection may affect the quality of the final visualization.

Another type of unsupervised learning seeks interesting correlations between variables in large datasets: association rule learning. Typically, it is used in an application field where one seeks to know the items that, in market basket analysis, are typically purchased together. The most well-known algorithm for learning association rules belongs to the Apriori method, which uses the generation of candidate itemsets and assessment of their support and confidence. While confidence is actually defined as a function of the probability that a transaction containing one item will also contain another, support is defined in terms of the relative frequency with which an itemset occurs in the dataset. Support and confidence together tend to discover strong association rules, thus guiding the placement of the products, marking tactics, and managing the inventory. Learning association rules can result in a very large number of rules, most of which would be weak or boring even though it can also result in insightful results. Techniques like threshold setting and rule trimming can be used to refine the results.

Another important technique under the umbrella of unsupervised learning is anomaly detection, which aims to find unusual patterns or outliers in the data. This method is especially valuable for application into many including quality assurance, fraud detection, and network security. In fact, one of the most common methods of anomaly identification is by application of clustering methods. An example of such a classification algorithm is the work of K-means and DBSCAN, an acronym that stands for Density-Based Spatial Clustering of Applications with Noise. The model can identify possible anomalies by grouping typical data points into clusters and finding out those that do not fit in well in one cluster. Alternately, the model can be trained to learn the normal distribution of the data and then pick out points that deviate from some predetermined threshold as anomalies. Realtime applications of anomaly detection often require the early identification of strange patterns to avert large losses or security breaches.

Unsupervised learning techniques have many benefits. Mainly, they allow one to analyze exploratory data without requiring labeled data, which often is difficult to access or expensive. Flexibility will enable practitioners to reveal hidden patterns and structures that may not be obtainable using more traditional forms of analysis. In addition, unsupervised learning techniques like feature extraction or dimensionality reduction when applied to pre-process data can immensely enhance the performance of the supervised learning techniques. However, unsupervised learning is also accompanied by several challenges. This being one of the major challenges whereby assessment of performance is difficult for the unsupervised models compared to supervised learning. It is easy to compute metrics like accuracy or F1-score on labeled data, but usually it is arbitrary and dependent on domain expertise when it comes to evaluating the quality of unsupervised models. It may have to go along with validation procedures either external or by visualization for determining how effective their models are.

Another area for improvement with unsupervised learning methods is that they tend to be noise-sensitive and prone to outliers. Noise introduces severe distortion into the results of dimensionality reduction or clustering algorithms. Because of this, it often causes false inferences to be drawn from them. Good data preparation techniques include feature selection, normalization, and outlier detection methods that reduce the impact of the said problem. Meaningful results are first obtained by ensuring integrity and purity in the data and, subsequently, using unsupervised learning techniques. An important limitation of unsupervised learning models is that they are difficult to interpret. Techniques of dimensionality reduction and clustering algorithms provide much insight into the data, but sometimes it is hard to understand the underlying reasons for certain patterns or groupings. Since decision-makers need to understand why certain results are likely based on the outputs, high-stakes applications may not be that useful for unsupervised learning approaches due to a lack of interpretability. Research continues to be done in how one can enhance the interpretability of unsupervised models so that results can be better communicated.

Considering these challenges, the field of unsupervised learning constitutes an expanding field with continuous breakthroughs and advancements. Researchers continue to explore new algorithms and techniques that make unsupervised learning methods more robust and effective. For example, advancements in deep learning have led to developing deep clustering algorithms, based upon which cluster performance can be improved utilizing the properties of a deep learning neural network. Various such techniques enable the discovery of sophisticated patterns of complex configurations in such high-dimensional data by harnessing the strengths of either traditional clustering methods or deep learning. Another increasing interest is shown toward incorporating unsupervised learning with other models of machine learning. With a range of labeled and unlabeled data, semi-supervised learning is a new concept that draws strengths from both supervised and unsupervised techniques. Including unsupervised learning into the training process will help practitioners improve the generalization power and performance of the supervised models.

In summary, unsupervised learning approaches are a very significant domain within the vast world of machine learning where researchers are allowed the opportunity to go through data, identify trends, and then come to well-informed conclusions without relying on some labeled result. Such techniques, from association rule learning to anomaly detection, clustering, and dimensionality reduction, provide insights that can support data-driven decision making in various sectors. Even with the challenges presented by the estimation of performance, noise management, and ensuring interpretability, unsupervised learning is becoming better owing to improvements and breakthroughs in its methods. No doubt the future of data analytics and machine learning will be shaped by the increasing relevance and impact of unsupervised learning approaches as organizations become more aware of the value of exploring and understanding data.

## Feature Engineering and Selection

Feature engineering as well as selection plays a very critical role in the machine learning pipeline, which gives a huge impact in how well predictive models do. These procedures involve choosing the most pertinent features that make the prediction capacity of the model even greater, as well as converting raw data into a format which algorithms can use efficiently. With the proliferation of machine learning applications in different sectors, it is very pertinent that the practitioners learn to create reliable models with accuracy. Feature engineering and selection are essential concepts that everyone should be familiar with. This section dissects the idea of feature engineering and selection, methods employed, the different uses of feature engineering and selections, the challenges involved, and the impact on model performance.

Feature engineering is the process of introducing new features or changing existing ones to make a machine learning algorithm better enabled to carry out its intended function. Of many, such techniques include mathematical transformation, combination of features, and creation of categorical variables from numerical data. Ultimately, the approach is fundamentally aimed at providing a model with thought-provoking inputs that capture the underlying pattern of data to be in a better position to enhance predictive power. For example, possibly the first features that were drawn for a batch of house price data might have been location, number of bedrooms, and square footage. Feature engineering could include the creation of new features like price per square foot or transforming the location variable into a machine learning-friendly one-hot encoded categorical variable.

Feature engineering can particularly be useful when the complexity of the underlying problem cannot be fully captured by the raw data. One common assumption in many machine learning algorithms, particularly when applying linear models, is the existence of some linear relationship between the input data and the output variables. Real-world connections are often more complex and nonlinear. Hence, engineers can create polynomial combinations of the features using methods like polynomial feature generation, which is the generation of polynomial combinations of existing characteristics or interaction terms. For instance, by including an interaction term in the sales prediction model, which folds the feature of sales revenue and marketing budget into one, the true impact of spending on sales can be completely captured. Feature engineering encompasses managing categorical variables as its component.

Categorical features such as gender or geography are very frequently encountered within data sets to represent different groups or categories. It is challenging for machine learning algorithms to deal with the kind of variable because it requires numerical input. Among the most popular approaches to solving this kind of issue is coding approach. As a result of one-hot encoding, that categorical data is transformed into binary variables, models can treat each category as different features. For example, if the data set includes a "color" variable with values red, blue, and green, one-hot encoding will result in the generation of three new binary features named is_red, is_blue, and is_green. This function offers the categorical data for algorithms that require numerical inputs but remains sorted under its category. Feature engineering is about creating and scaling features.

If the feature has distinct ranges or units of measurement, then feature scaling is really important because the scale of input data has a drastic impact on most algorithms in machine learning. There are two most common methods of feature scaling; these include normalization and standardization. Normally, normalization rescales the features so that they lie within a particular range for most cases, such as [0, 1]. Standardization is the re-scaling of characteristics so that they have a mean of zero and a standard deviation of one. Feature scaling accelerates the optimization algorithm's convergence and makes the model more efficient because it allows all features to participate in the training of the model equally. Although feature selection focuses on the selection of relevant features, which have increased the model's ability to predict based on that selected feature, feature engineering tries to enhance the model's input data.

Good feature selection can also bring other benefits such as reduced overfitting, lower computational cost, and improved model interpretation. Feature selection is one of the essential procedures in dealing with high-dimensional data where the number of features may be much higher than the number of observations. In some circumstances, a large number of features may contain unnecessary or redundant data that will negatively impact the performance of the model. Three broad categories of methods are possible for feature selection: filter methods, wrapper methods, and embedding methods. Filter approaches use statistical metrics and criteria to evaluate the significance of features with no machine learning algorithm. Chi-square tests, mutual information, and correlation coefficients are typical examples. For instance, a learner may determine the relationship of each attribute with the target variable in a multivariate dataset and proceed by selecting only those attributes that have a high degree of correlation. Although filter methods are intuitive and cheap computationally, it ignores interactions between attributes as well as the particular predictive model. Wrapper methods, on the other hand, use an explicit learning algorithm to estimate the performance of multiple subsets of features.

These algorithms function based on the criteria of addition or removal of features for models, using their performance measures. Some common ones include recursive feature elimination, forward selection, and backward elimination. While backward elimination begins with all the features in place and removes them iteratively based on their contribution towards the development of the model, forward selection starts with an empty feature set by adding features one at a time. The approaches embedded incorporate feature selection into the model's training process. Wrapper methods, again with all this focus placed on the specific model, usually bring better accuracy results but can be computationally very expensive, especially with high-dimensional features. Examples of these approaches include ridge regression and other types of regularization, like LASSO (Least Absolute Shrinkage and Selection Operator). LASSO introduces a penalty term to the loss function, which encourages sparsity in the model coefficients and will thus set some of those coefficients to zero in order to select a subset of features. In this way, practitioners can choose automatically features as a model is fitted. Ridge regression introduces another penalty term; however, in this case, rather than forcing all the coefficients to zero, it penalizes the magnitudes. When developing a model, embedded techniques constitute an effective alternative in order to select features with a balanced approach between the filter and wrapper methods. Feature engineering, beside the model performance, also plays a critical role.

These processes make the model more interpretable and understandable. In most applications, stakeholders need to know how particular features influence predictions. A good practitioner constructs models that generate accurate predictions and clear interpretations of the same by careful selection of relevant features and engineering illustrative inputs. Thus, in a model predicting patient outcomes, for example, in the healthcare industry, it highlights crucial characteristics such as age, medical history, and lifestyle factors, which enable doctors to base their decisions on the recommendations made by the model. There are some practical challenges, even with the advantages of feature engineering and selection.

One of the significant problems is that it could lead to over-engineering features, wherein the complexity of the engineered characteristics may cause overfitting. It is stated that overfitting occurs when a model learns noise from the training data rather than the underlying patterns. Reducing this risk calls for practices in which a model is to be validated well on unseen data by use of cross-validation and ensuring a proper balance between interpretability and model complexity since overly complex models are hard to explain to stakeholders. A further challenge is that feature engineering and selection involve much computational cost, particularly with large datasets or high-dimensional feature spaces. The time and resources consumed in the processes of feature selection and engineering may become unaffordable as the number of features increases. AutoML frees up practitioners to focus on analyzing and applying the findings by streamlining these processes and providing practitioners with effective solutions for feature engineering and selection.

Recent advances in deep learning have also reached feature engineering and selection. Deep neural networks have the ability to automatically discover features from raw data, thereby avoiding time-consuming human feature engineering. Nevertheless, deep learning models are often difficult to interpret because they usually tend to act as black boxes. Emerging techniques include SHAP (SHapley Additive exPlanations) and layer-wise relevance propagation, which help open up the model's workings as well as expose which features are important. Good feature design and selection apply across the board in all machine learning paradigms, but deep learning can automate parts of feature engineering. Automation and domain knowledge will most likely be incorporated in feature engineering and selection in the future.

In order to accelerate the feature generation process and also to enable practitioners to explore even more transformations and combinations easily, automated feature engineering tools and algorithms are now being designed. Also, because domain expertise can influence feature design and selection tactics, collaboration between data scientists and domain experts is in need. Through the integration of knowledge from domain-specific fields and data science, practitioners may develop more robust models to solve real-world problems in a more efficient way. In brief, feature engineering and selection play important roles in the machine learning process with a great effect on how well predictive models work, how easy to understand, and how applicable they will be.

Feature engineering and selection, which transforms unstructured data into meaningful features and then makes choices that are most pertinent inputs, can help professionals enhance the prediction capability of their models and provide them with valuable insights toward decision-making. Here are some of the offered methods for optimizing model performance by feature engineering and selection strategies: filtering, encoding, scaling, clustering, and wrapper methods. Issues such as overfitting, computational costs, and even interpretability need to be resolved for its successful implementation. The input of automation with domain expertise in feature engineering/selection will hugely impact data-driven decision making across all sectors as machine learning continues to advance.

## Model Evaluation and Tuning

Developing a model in the domain of machine learning is half of the process and the other is the evaluation and fine-tuning of the developed model so it could operate at its optimum. So, the half thus model evaluation and tuning are the key steps of the machine learning process that help analyze the predictability of algorithms besides improving their performance. This section discusses the significance of model evaluation and tuning as well as how critically important the methods and measurements a person applies in these procedures are, and additionally, the hardships and problems that practitioners have to encounter while producing positive results.

Model evaluation is the process of determining how well a machine learning model performs on a given dataset. Hence, overfitting, biasing a model, it would produce an unbiased estimate of how the model would behave on simulated data so that users might understand how the model might act in reality. Overfitting is actually one of the errors during model evaluation, where the learned model picks up too many patterns-noise and outliers from the training data-so it needs to generalize better on new data. To reduce this risk, practitioners have to use robust methods for evaluation such that they express appropriately the generalization capability of the model.

The most common technique of model evaluation is called train-test split. This technique divides a dataset into two subsets. It is in the test set where the model is tested and the training set where the model will be trained upon. This is done in this manner such that division occurs randomly and thereby the two sets are representative of the entire dataset. Usually, it is evaluated on the hidden test set after it has been seen how well the model has learnt after passing through the training set. However, at times this approach may result in a false positive especially when the size of the dataset is low or when the split fails to capture all the richness of the data it represents. To counter such problems, practitioners often turn to cross-validation techniques.

In cross-validation, we basically split the existing dataset into folds or subsets. Then, we train our model on some of it and validate that on remaining folds. It is pretty much a powerful method, where multiple repetitions of this process ensure every fold gets used as a validation set at least once. The most commonly used cross-validation technique is k-fold cross-validation, which applies k folds of the same size in a data set. In so doing, one trains a model k times using one fold as a validation set and the rest as the training set. This approach reduces the randomness attributed to a single train-test split and rather leads to a stable estimate of the performance of the model. A proper assessment of the performance of the model is achieved through an average of all the k iterations.

Relevant criteria, in the assessment of performance, should be used in the quantification and such criteria should relate to the specific goals of the job at hand. It depends on the statistic used to determine how well a model performs for performance evaluation. Classification has a number of common evaluation metrics, which are F1-score, recall, accuracy, and precision. Accuracy occurs when the model correctly predicts the entire test sets. A caveat about accuracy is that it might mislead in a situation where the class distribution of the data is unbalanced, meaning that one class is greatly represented over the other. In such situations, precision, recall, and F1 score are more informative. Recall is the percentage of true positives out of all real positives, whereas precision is the percentage of true positive forecasts out of all the positive prediction made. The F1 score is another statistic with a balance between precision and recall calculated by the harmonic mean of both.

There are a number of metrics which examine the model on regression tasks. Some very common regression metrics include R-squared, Mean Squared Error (MSE), and Mean Absolute Error (MAE). MAE measures the average absolute difference between actual and projected values as an interpreted indicator of prediction accuracy. The average squared difference, or MSE, calculates the difference of two values and weighs the higher errors more. R-squared tells one how good the fit of the model is by calculating the percent of variance that can be explained from the dependent variable through the independent variables. The choice of metrics is a matter of difference in the interpretation of the results and helps with tweaking. Something else that needs to be done following testing for a model is fine-tuning it towards further improvement of the model's performance. Model tuning is, in some context, known as hyperparameter optimization. This gives the alteration of the hyperparameters that exists in the model for improvement of its performance on the validation set. Hyperparameters are the pre-defined settings, which are not utilized during the process of training data. They are involved in determining regularization, the learning rate, complexity of the model, and other related features of a model. For example, in decision trees, the hyperparameters may be minimum no. samples to split an internal node or maximum depth which would hugely impact the behavior of the model.

Hyperparameter tuning can also be performed using grid search and even random search along with more complex methods involving Bayesian optimization. It performs a grid search over each of the specified ranges for the respective hyperparameters. This means providing a range of values for each and every hyperparameter, and then going through an intensive analysis of all the possible combinations of these hyperparameters in order to determine the best performing set. Grid search certainly gives the ideal results; however, this can be computationally very expensive due to large numbers of parameters or very wide ranges. In contrast, random search allows for an even more efficient means of searching over hyperparameter space using random samples of combinations of hyperparameters sampled from specified distributions. In general, it ends with highly competitive solutions in significantly shorter time, although it only sometimes results in the ideal blend.

Bayesian optimization is yet another state-of-the-art hyperparameter optimization technique. Probabilistic models are utilized for guiding the search for the optimal hyperparameters. A surrogate model is used in building the approximation of objective function performance - a basis for how to sample next in the hyperparameter space. Since this is fundamentally an exploration-exploitation trade-off, the approach is best suited to expensive objectives. Bayesian Optimization can discover the optimal or very nearly optimal hyperparameters in fewer evaluations where a focus is put on very promising areas leading to better results.

Model tweaking and testing is an important job, but to be aware of possible dangers the practitioner has to remember. Overfitting occurs when over-tuning hyperparameters and is a serious concern specially if one is tuning with training data. Keeping test, validation, and training sets separate is very essential in order to avoid overfitting. Then, the test set will come last time in evaluating the model's performance; the training set will be used in training the model, and the validation set will be used in performing the tune of the hyperparameters. This split ensures that the model will be tested on truly unseen data, thereby giving a better approximation of its generalization capabilities. Yet another challenge in the evaluation and fine-tuning of the models is the issue of "leakage," that is, the unintended leakage from the test or validation sets to the training process. Leakage may lead to optimistically biased performance estimates, which then translates to poor model performance in real-world situations. Hence, experiments must be designed carefully to avoid bias through uniform use of feature engineering, data transformation, and pretreatment techniques on training, validation, and test sets.

Model evaluation and tuning is an iterative process of iteration and improvement. Undoubtedly it's not a one-time activity. The model may have to be retrained and reevaluated based on the new data coming in, which will preserve their goodness for the prediction. The continuous need for assessment therefore calls for the need to have a good monitoring system that traces performance changes of the model over time. The underlying pattern within the data might change, hence causing performance drift. For such reasons, models must be continually under check and updates to trace the current situation, thus keeping the models correct. Yet further considerations in model evaluations are added by rising interest in interpretability and fairness in machine learning models. Practitioners have to make choices about when models work well enough for a particular demographic group without continuing or perpetuating existing biases or perpetuating inequity. Some interpretability frameworks and tools have been developed to make practitioners better understand how the model produces predictions by gaining insight into feature importance and model behavior, as is the case with the use of SHAP values and LIME: Local Interpretable Model-agnostic Explanations.

The two key elements involved in the machine learning workflow, namely, model evaluation and adjustment, have a very important influence on the effectiveness and use of predictive models. Using such sound assessment strategies, proper selection of performance metrics, and efficient tweaking of hyperparameters, practitioners are today capable of designing models that display good generalization to data already seen. However, there are issues of overfitting, leakage, and constant monitoring that need careful consideration to be sure of satisfactory results. Advances in machine learning will ensure the evaluation and tuning of the model put emphasis on interpretability and fairness; this ensures applications of predictive models as useful tools for decision-making across a wide variety of applications. In fact, all will access full potential in machine learning through employment of the best possible techniques for assessment and adjustment, thus unlocking creativity and understanding into many relevant sectors.

# CHAPTER IV

# Advanced Topics in Machine Learning

## Deep Learning Overview

Deep learning is one of the subset machine learning technologies that has, in the last few years, propelled breakthroughs in almost all fields - particularly in robotics, computer vision, natural language processing, and speech recognition. Large volumes of data, increased processing power, and sophisticated algorithms allow models of deep learning to extract intricate patterns from data-all factors that have contributed to its explosive rise. An overview of deep learning is provided in this section, discussing its underlying theories, architectures, uses, and current obstacles.

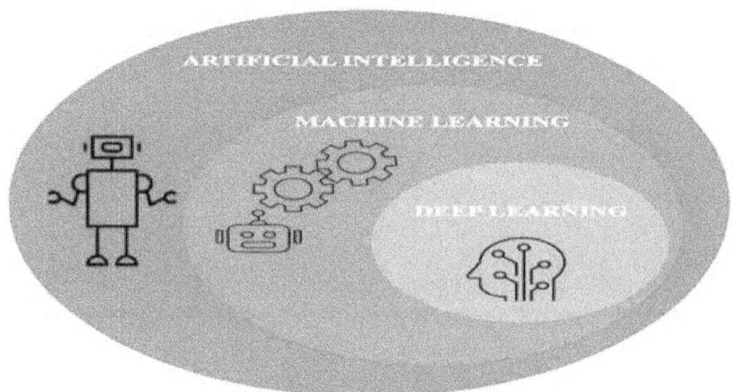


Deep learning uses bases in the form of artificial neural networks; simply put, computer models modeled after those found within an animal's brain in biological neural networks. These neural networks are composed of layered nodes or "neurons" that are interconnected with each other. Each layer takes input after a transformation and then sends the outcome to the next layer. The use of several layers—hence the word "deep"—enables the model to learn hierarchical representations of data, which is the big idea behind deep learning. Generally, deeper layers have captured more abstract and higher-level features, but the earliest layers have accumulated lower-level features. In image processing, for example, top layers might be concerned with textures and edges, while lower layers might be concerned with objects and detailed patterns.

The architectures of deep learning models can be highly task and input dependent. CNNs are very commonly used in tasks involving images since they automatically detect and learn spatial hierarchies in images. Adding filters to the input data allows convolutional layers, which CNNs apply, to focus on local patterns and characteristics. This localization makes CNNs remarkably excellent in tasks like segmentation, object detection, and picture classification. However, RNNs are suitable for applications such as time series analysis and natural language processing because they are designed keeping sequential input in mind. RNNs allow the model to find relationships in terms of time through storing information about earlier inputs via a feedback loop technique. LSTM networks are a special type of RNN, designed to increase the capacity for learning more distant dependencies to overcome the vanishing gradient problem.

Availability of large amounts of data is one of the major reasons why deep learning was able to gain momentum. Traditional methods for many applications required handcrafted features based on rich domain knowledge during their training process, which limited their capabilities and applications. Big data has made it possible for learning-based deep models to learn enormous datasets for automatic representation and feature extraction with less manual human input. Such a skill has revolutionized many domains with great innovation. For example, computer vision models trained on millions of tagged images were said to be at par with humans when it came to image classification and object detection. An important growth factor for deep learning has been rapid advances in computing power, particularly in the use of Graphics Processing Units. Because of a very high degree of parallelization, GPUs can execute the matrix operations needed for deep learning algorithms. Researchers and practitioners can train very complex deep learning models much faster using GPUs than on conventional CPUs. Thus, this acceleration allows now to explore deeper and more complex neural networks in the scope of tasks of performance boosts.

Additional contributors for making deep learning technologies accessible to a larger group of users are deep learning frameworks and libraries-PyTorch, Keras, and TensorFlow. With user-friendly interfaces and pre-built features, plus optimized implementations, this makes developing, training, and deploying deep learning models easier for researchers and developers to utilize. The resulting new structures and methods that have produced increased experimentation and innovation in the system triggered by this accessibility have made a better way to extend the limits of what deep learning is capable of.

Deep learning has unlocked possibilities and transformed many industries. Deep learning algorithms have, therefore, been applied in the health sector through the analysis of radiological images to enhance the analysis of medical images and diagnose diseases such as cancer. Such models provide profound insights and even help in diagnosis by spotting minute patterns that a human radiologist would not notice. Deep learning has also been very well applied in drug discovery, focusing on the optimization of chemical compounds and predicting molecular interactions, to mention a few. All this would therefore be a considerable increase in research speed and development.

Deep learning has revolutionized the natural language processing domain in that it first of all changes how machines comprehend and generate human language. Popular designs such as BERT and GPT are based on models like Transformers that have performed spectacularly well in language understanding tasks, including tasks such as sentiment analysis, language translation, and text production. Using attention mechanisms for example, these models of capturing relationships and also their contexts within texts facilitate more precise as well as coherent language processing.

Deep learning has also recently made tremendous breakthroughs in autonomous systems, including robotics and the self-driving car. Deep reinforcement learning emerges as a synergy between reinforcement learning and deep learning, permitting agents to learn optimal behaviors based on interaction with their environment. The approach of the program was thus demonstrated in the context of teaching a self-driving car how to navigate through all those tricky situations and make snap decisions in real-time based on sensory data. These technologies will eventually revolutionize whole industries and the relationship of people with machines as they develop.

Deep learning is also not without its set of problems. Huge, labelled datasets are one of the biggest challenges among them. Though deep models are excellent at learning from enormous volumes of data, gathering labelled data can be costly and time-consuming. Expert labeling is a prerequisite for producing high-quality annotated datasets across multiple domains, such as finance and healthcare, which actually poses a bottleneck in training these models. Researchers are interested in approaches like transfer learning and semi-supervised learning that directly target this problem. Semi-supervised learning enables the model to learn from a much larger set of available data by making use of both labeled and unlabeled data. In contrast, transfer learning reduces the amount of labeled data needed for efficient training through pre-training a model on a large dataset then refining it on a smaller, task-specific dataset. Another challenge is that the interpretability of deep learning models decreases as the models grow deeper and more complex. End. These challenges come in the midst of all those sectors-the health sector, banking, and even law-based sectors-where transparency is crucial. Researchers are developing methods to illustrate decision boundaries, highlight important features, and explain their predictive results to make the deep learning model more readable. Thus, interpretable models are a way to win over stakeholders and assure responsible implementation in practical applications.

Another common criticism of the deep learning model is high energy and computation. Deep neural networks require a lot of processing power to train them, which is a problem in the use of much energy during lengthy training processes. Along with the demand for deep learning applications, growing needs for more energy-efficient algorithms and hardware that could offer performance without wasting energy are growing. This led to research efforts in methods such as model pruning, quantization, and knowledge distillation for producing smaller, faster, and more resource-efficient models. There have been, in recent years, some recognition and emphasis among the deep learning community on ethical issues while using AI technology. Issues of justice, accountability, and prejudice have become far more apparent within the context of deep learning since the algorithms utilized therein can sometimes unwittingly amplify and even reinforce the biases already present in the training data. It should have a multiple layered strategy that would go beyond curating datasets in the proper manner by designing bias detection techniques and actively monitoring real-world applications' performance of deep models. Ethical issues can thus come to the forefront to help researchers and practitioners ascertain that these technologies are developed and deployed ethically.

Many trends and orientations are influencing the future of deep learning as it's further developed. However, an important trend is deep learning's seepage into other disciplines: physics, biology, and social science. More and more researchers are turning towards deep learning to solve a daunting problem in other fields by taking its ability to draw insightful conclusions from a wide array of data sources. For example, deep learning is used in astrophysics for the recognition of celestial objects and phenomena from large volumes of scientific data. Other developments include self- and unsupervised-supervised learning strategies that are related to reduced reliance on labeled data. These methods open up new avenues for the training of deep learning models in settings where required labeled data is elusive to be obtained because it allows models to learn representations from their data without requiring explicit annotations. Self-supervised learning has received much attention recently in natural language processing because it provides models with the possibility of learning from large samples of text with minimal annotations. The following methods have the potential to significantly expand the applications of deep learning into a wide range of fields.

Future technological advancements in hardware and architectures will also play a role in deep learning's future. The full change that will be brought about by high technologies such as neuromorphic computing and quantum computing is expected to fully revolutionize training and the application of deep learning models. Neuromorphic computing targets the creation of models designed to be more powerful and efficient, imitating the composition and manner of operations in the human brain, neuromorphic computing models computers as being tenfold better for intricate computations than standard computers. Quantum Computing promises much towards increased possibilities for deep learning applications since it can execute intricate computations ten times faster than regular computers.

In summary, deep learning has been the front-runner of modern artificial intelligence, which had gained an excellent number of discoveries in several fields. With its key principal of neural network design, large datasets, and powerful computational resources, it is the driving force behind its wide-scale success in picture and audio recognition to natural language processing and autonomous systems. Deep learning is now being increasingly used across multiple fields but is always out of its challenges in data requirements, interpretability, efficiency, and recently with ethical considerations. Research and innovation in the future will face these issues. The shape of what artificial intelligence shall become and how it will have an impact upon society is defined and sure to turn out grand because artificial intelligence already can overthrow whole sectors and also enhance human capacities as it continues to develop. If one acknowledges and addresses all these problems accompanying the power of deep learning, researchers and practitioners may safely and effectively use the power of deep learning.

## Natural Language Processing

The core objective of the NLP field belonging to the computer science and artificial intelligence or AI field is that computers can interact with human languages in some way by making machines produce, understand, and interpret human language in a useful and significant way. NLP is a very broad field, including numerous approaches and strategies that enable computers to process and analyze tremendous amounts of natural language input, which makes machine communication possible. Therefore, this section spans foundational concepts in natural language processing, its diverse applications, challenges, and opportunities in the field.

Actually, it originated from a hybrid of language study and computer science, named computational linguistics. The early approaches toward NLP were based upon rule-based techniques; with these techniques, the linguists would specify the syntax and grammatical rules for a given language. Unfortunately, these systems were often severely constrained by the vagary and complexity involved in human languages. And hence, research in statistical methods began by making good use of huge corpora in the extraction of patterns and relationships within the languages. This, in turn, brought the paradigm shift in natural language processing towards more complex algorithms and models that could learn from data rather than just being a rule-following algorithm.

The other history of the current state of natural language processing is said to be related to the advent of machine learning which led to shifting handling of linguistic data in entirely new directions. Machine learning applies mathematical techniques to make it possible for an algorithm to learn from examples, thus pinpointing patterns and structures that exist in the linguistic data. Therefore, along with the development of supervised learning that consists in the training of models on labeled data, this methodology becomes increasingly popular as a method of text classification, named entity recognition, and sentiment analysis. Such approaches did show seeming performance improvements and thus precipitated the wider use of NLP in other domains.

Better NLP tools are ever more pressing needs considering explosive growth in the internet domain and growth in textual information. Possibly, the most direct application of NLP has to do with information retrieval and extraction. NLP offers a means to interpret the queries submitted by search engines like Google and to return the results accordingly. NLP enables the search engine to return substantially more precise and insightful results to the users by reviewing the context and semantics of phrases searched for. Some more applications of NLP include extracting meaningful information from sources that are unstructured such as posts on social media, customer reviews, and replies to surveys with the purpose of discovering customers' attitudes and preferences. Another very famously known application is machine translation, an automatic translation between languages. That is translating a given text by a computer from one language into another. Traditionally, rule-based algorithms in translation rarely manage to replicate the subtleties of spoken languages and contexts of words. Good-quality translations have much improved with the advent of statistical machine translation and more recently, neural machine translation. Now, neural machine translation models process whole sentences using deep learning techniques rather than the traditional systems that used individual words, making the output much more fluid and appropriate in context.

Another area NLP has leaped is that of conversational agents, or better known as chatbots. Chatbots are the virtual assistants that interact with customers in natural language as they simultaneously provide real-time support and information. They can recognize user queries and provide relevant responses based on techniques such as NLP techniques ranging from entity extraction and intent identification. They can be used in the following applications: virtual shopping assistants, customer assistance systems, and personal productivity aids. NLP is constantly upgrading the brains of chatbots, as they can reply to complex questions and also respond to various other questions personally, learn from interaction, and much more.

Another use of NLP is sentiment analysis. Sentiment analysis means the emotional undertone of a given document. Even companies can detect the general mood about their product or service by analyzing the feedback obtained from their customers through social media, product reviews, or voting. The emotions can be classified as positive, negative, or neutral using an algorithm in machine learning. It avails long-term insights about the production process and marketing strategy also. Even companies can construe the public opinion and alter their planning accordingly. It is used in political analysis, brand monitoring and social media management.

NLP is now one of the high-growth technologies; even though progress is really fast the problems still exist for NLP to score 100%. The first problem originates from the complexity of language sources and vagueness; most words have multiple meanings, phrases are ambiguous according to a context, and idiomatic expressions can mislead algorithms processing them. Example: The phrase "to kick the bucket" is related to death but also an object; NLP systems fail in such nuances because they learn data and a context and have to distinguish hundreds of possible meanings. Failure of NLP models: Most languages need more high-quality labeled datasets. While many sources are available in English, there exists a much more limited representation in several other languages. This makes it difficult to train reliable models for other languages. In addition, simplified NLP techniques easily get blocked while processing such as a Finnish or Turkish language because of its complexities in morphology. Due to this fact, it is hence important to study unsupervised and semi-supervised learning strategies whereby the model learns from unannotated data or somehow makes better use of amounts of labeled data.

Ethics considerations are equally important in NLP. Training large corpora text modeling could learn biases present within the data; these would then cause problems in an application like content control, law enforcement or hiring for example by generating a biased output from a language model that has been trained on a biased input. Hence, such ethical consideration deserves proper attention at the time of data collection and model training. Two of the most commonly researched approaches that cancel bias and ensure models with no bias for NLP applications are adversarial training and debiasing. Transformer-based architectures revolutionize natural language processing and transform the totality of work. Data sequences go through transformer architecture using self-attentions as first proposed in Vaswani et al. seminal "Attention is All You Need". This architecture overcomes the weakness of recurrent neural networks by enabling models to capture the relation between words regardless of where they are in a sentence. Transfer learning has been epitomized by effectiveness of many initially pre-trained models in the applications of natural language processing such as BERT and GPT that have set a new bar of performance in industries. Such models can be tuned to specific tasks and give excellent performance on large datasets that are capable of performing research and development.

Some new innovations affect the way NLP is developed. The most popular one is the recent trend of multimodal processing, where the model resorts to contextual knowledge from more than one modality, such as text, image, and audio. Such multimodal models are going to intuitively become better understood in the context and meaning because such data coming from multiple sources builds them, leading to richer interactions and more sophisticated applications. Further, applications where models need to interpret visual as well as textual input, like in the applications of picture captioning and that of visual question answering, will be further enhanced with the integration of NLP and computer vision.

Low-resource languages and methods to devise highly efficient NLP models without requiring huge, labeled datasets is another trend. This domain of work has thrown into the limelight numerous new techniques that flourish in the glare of zero-shot and few-shot learning, where models are to be trained to accomplish tasks using little or no labeled samples. Such approaches tend to be targeted at bringing the benefit of natural language processing to languages and domains, that so far still need to be more adequately represented due to the dearth of available resources. A future of NLP lies in a more critical investigation into ethical issues. The wide dissemination of NLP technologies shall make systems increasingly more transparent and responsible. By demanding the creation of frameworks and guidelines that guarantee responsible AI development, researchers raise greater importance of user privacy, fairness, and transparency for NLP applications. The NLP community may search for the creation of systems that respect users' rights and facilitate equitable outcomes by putting the first priority on the issues that are fundamentally ethical.

Most of the growth in NLP is likely from better hardware and computation capacity. Specialized hardware has started to propel forward efficiency and scalability in NLP models, starting with tensors processing units and neural network accelerators. As researchers come up with new products through the expansion of computational capacity, they may train bigger, even more complex models; there is still new opportunity and capability. NLP is a very dynamic and fast-developing domain which allows the robot to understand the human language ability and get engaged in it. It has used machine learning approaches to develop textual communication in technology, elaborating complex models on different applications; however, the issues about prejudice, ambiguity, poor quality of data, and ethical concerns in the main areas of consideration remain. It has witnessed revolution with the advent of transformer-based models and has given rise to considerable performance gains on many tasks. Future for NLP in the near future would be determined by incorporating multimodal processing, investigating low-resource languages, and placing more emphasis on the ethics to be found in hand. Therefore, approaches towards such problems and proper usage of the capabilities of natural language processing can be a source for opening up new ways of human-to-machine interaction and improve our perception about language in the new age.

## Time Series Analysis

It's a statistical method called time series analysis that is used in examining data points gathered or recorded at specific periods of time. In fact, understanding patterns across time can provide important insights and guide decision-making in lots of sectors: environmental science, engineering, economics, and finance, to name a few. And thus, it's quite important. Time series data, because the trends, seasonality, cyclic behavior, and erratically fluctuating situations occur very often, should be analyzed and interpreted with proper methods. The basic ideas of time series analysis have been presented in this section while its methods, uses, problems, and possible future developments are included.

Basically, time series analysis refers to the study of sequences of data points that have been collected at different times. Such points represent measurements regarding stock prices, temperature readings, and economic indicators, among other variables tracked over extensive periods of time. The primary aim of time series analysis lies in the identification of any potential underlying trends, patterns, or relationships within data from which analysts can then use historical observations to predict futures better and make informed judgments.

Having identified them, stakeholders could better plan and allocate their resources, predict potential future effects, and leverage tactics to their best extent.

The most significant role of time series analysis in breaking down time series data is its component parts. Data on time series appears in four general parts: irregular fluctuations, seasonality, cyclic patterns, and trends. This would mean that the trend component indicates change within the data over time and may point out whether a variable is rising, falling, or stable. Therefore, it may be used to predict stock movement, how the overall firm grew in value, and also the value placed on the company by the market. The term "seasonality" refers to predictable patterns that occur weekly, monthly, or yearly. Factors outside the organization's influence that often influence the pattern include seasons, holidays, and economic cycles. For instance, retail sales are likely to have seasonality since most sales tend to peak during holiday periods. Analysts can account for these expected variations within their estimates by determining and measuring these seasonal effects.

However, cyclic patterns are not time-locked or because of business/economic cycles that often affect them. These cycles go for many years and portray more fundamental trends of the economy, such as an expansion and then a contraction. For instance, cyclical real estate trends may exist, and property values may grow and then decline because of changes in interest rates, economic conditions, and even consumers' confidence. Often termed "noise," such irregularities represent random fluctuations in time series data that cannot be isolated and separated from the effects of seasonality, business cycles, or trends. Natural disasters, economic shocks, and a change in policy can make or break a calculated notion so rendered by such an analysis. Anomalies should, therefore, be included in such an analysis to prevent misleading conclusions about the underlying patterns of the data.

Time series data analysis requires that one uses a combination of approaches and techniques. Descriptive statistics forms the simplest method for providing insights into the distribution, dispersion, and central tendency of the data at hand. Analysts will usually compute measures like mean, median, standard deviation, and range for an easy summary of time series data, which makes cross-temporal comparisons possible. Another very common technique is moving averages, which help smooth out short-term fluctuations by averaging data points over a specific time period. Through its capacity to allow the tracing of trends and patterns within time series data, moving averages free analysts from noise in the short term while helping focus on the underlying behavior. Depending on what would be achieved with an investigation, variations of moving average, such as simple moving average and exponential moving average, can be used.

The ARIMA models are very frequently used in time series analysis. The future values in the historical observations are estimated as this model of ARIMA combines moving averages, differencing, and autoregression—where present values rely on prior values. This makes the data stationary. Therefore, if data contains autocorrelation or between past and future values, it is of much help. The accuracy of the prediction can be improved by changing the parameters of ARIMA models to get the best fit to the data.

In addition to ARIMA, the STL is another useful approach. Breaking down a time series into three different components-trend, seasonal, and residuals-allows analysts to gain deeper understanding of what happens at the underlying dynamics. This method is especially useful when dealing with seasonal data that may have complex seasonality patterns as it separates out many different factors. This makes it possible to do a better job of forecasting. Time series analysis was found to exhibit a growing trend of machine learning techniques in recent years. Machine learning algorithms are more adept at handling the gigantic nature of datasets and capturing non-linear patterns than traditional statistical models, which often assume linear correlations and require stationary data. Time series forecasting has shown spectacular performance from methods like recurrent neural networks, or Long Short-Term Memory (LSTM) networks. This is because LSTMs learn long-term relationships and handle sequential data, making them highly applicable in time series datasets that contain complex patterns and anomalies.

Applications for time series analysis are very broad and cut across diverse sectors and fields. In finance, it mostly involves the evaluation of risk involved in investment, analysis of market trends, and short-term forecasting for stock prices. Time series analysis forms a very significant tool that investors employ in the course of unearthing historic trends and knowing how best to manage their portfolios. For instance, traders can use technical indicators such as moving averages derived from time series analysis to find when it's best to enter or leave the financial markets. A valuable tool for the economists in studying economic variables such as inflation, GDP and unemployment rates by identifying patterns and cycles can assess success programs and create projections that guide economic strategy, tracking these indicators over time. For instance, a central bank uses time-series analysis when considering inflationary patterns while changing the interest rates to keep the economy stable.

Time series analysis is also applied for research into the environment, in particular for natural resources management and climate change. Researchers follow a time track of temperature and precipitation and other environmental data to establish trends and patterns that may lead to elements guiding conservation efforts and policy decisions. Time series can be used to analyze effects from human activities on ecosystems as well as identify long-term climate changes. Time series analysis is also crucial in supply chain management and demand forecasting. Companies can control their inventories and the production of their company's policies using time series techniques for estimating client demand on their products or services. Reliable demand forecasts enable companies to minimize waste, avoid wastage, and increase customer satisfaction through ensuring that products are available at the right time when required.

Time series analysis has many applications and advantages but has weaknesses, which may make its application in forecasting and explanation difficult. One of the main difficulties of dealing with missing data arising from various reasons, such as equipment malfunction or data collection problems or irregular time intervals between observations. More data is needed to ensure the accuracy of the forecasts and deliver biased results. Missing data estimations are usually accounted for using interpolation or imputation methods; however, the use of those methods has to be weighed out since too many can lead to distortion.

Another issue is the presence of outliers in time series data. Outliers skew results and, hence, might distort the results and, thus, analysis. It implies that there is a requirement to identify and handle the outliers so that the analysis of time series is robust. Identification of outliers can be done with the aid of various statistical tests and visualization methods; with their support, the decision is made either to retain or modify or exclude them from the dataset. This is also worth paying attention to the stationarity assumption in time series analysis. Many classical methods require data to be steady, or with statistical characteristics that do not change over time.

Conversely, most of the real world time series are non-stationary, that means either their trends or seasonality shift over time. To address this issue, analysts often apply transformations so as to make the data stationary before carrying out further analysis, differencing or detrending.

Given the rapid pace of change in technology, data access, and analytical techniques, time series analysis can expect a radical outcome in the future. The enormous volume and variability of time series data generated across industries have grown exponentially with the growth of big data and the Internet of Things. Since businesses are embracing this level of data, advanced time series analysis methodologies will increasingly be in demand. Further, advancements in machine learning and artificial intelligence for application in time series analysis are anticipated to be more comprehensive and therefore produce more profound insights from complex data. With the power of machine learning algorithms, there can be improvements on efficient realization of time series analysis through automated forecasting systems which would enable real-time predictions and models that adapt self-actively to change conditions.

In addition, time series analysis tool and software, which will be user friendly, will make these methods more accessible to those non-experts, and thus a higher number of people will be able to make use of time series analysis's benefit while making their decisions. With growing comprehension of the importance of data-based insights at the companies and organizations, time series analysis will become much more important for planning and maximizing results.

In a nutshell, time series analysis is one of the most informative statistical techniques that provides knowledge about some data that has been taken over such a long period. Breaking down time series data into its components and using numerous techniques, analysts can show patterns, trends, and even correlations guiding the decisions in so many spheres. Technological advances, the widespread acceptance of machine learning, and continuing advances in analytical techniques will be the chief drivers of the future of time series analysis. Moreover, other more diverse problems, such as missing data, outliers, and non-stationarity, although certainly cumbersome in their own right, will also gradually recede as abilities improve to evaluate and make sense of the huge volumes of time-stamped data firms continue to generate and collect. Strategy creation in a rapidly growing data-driven environment is becoming increasingly dependent upon maximizing performance.

## Reinforcement Learning

Reinforcement learning is a very powerful paradigm of machine learning, capable of learning to act in an agent which possibly maximizes the cumulative reward in a given environment. This is fundamentally different from the supervised learning model where models learn from labeled datasets; instead, reinforcement learning makes use of an idea called trial and error. The strategy of the agent improves with time due to its learning through action in some environment and receiving feedback either as incentives or penalties. In this section, reinforcement learning is discussed along with its algorithms, uses, difficulties, and potential future developments. The basic idea applied in reinforcement learning has an agent that interacts with an environment. The agent perceives the status of the environment as it is and acts in ways that can potentially change it. To the agent, feedback from the environment would be incentives that tell the agent how well its taken actions were appreciated. Hence, for an agent, the main goal would then be to construct a policy or a mapping from states to actions that maximizes the predicted cumulative reward over time. This process of learning from experience in interactions is generally incorporated under the name Markov Decision Process. In this MDP, the next state will depend on the present state and action and cannot be specified based on a sequence of past events.

A few of the major concepts or building blocks of reinforcement learning under this big umbrella include States, Actions, Rewards, and Policies. States represent all of the many possible configurations that the environment could be in. States change over time according to the actions performed by an agent, and all of the different game possibilities of placing a chess player's pieces on a board represent every state in a game of chess. The actions of the agent within each state are called actions, and the numerical values that function as representations of rewards provide information to the agent regarding how well those choices worked. The work of an agent is to come up with an optimal policy that specifies what to do in every condition in order to maximize the overall expected reward.

The most basic concept of reinforcement learning is Exploration vs Exploitation. The agent needs to balance exploitation, taking advantages known to work with a high potential reward and exploration, investigation of new acts to learn their prospective rewards. This will fail to take the best action that may result in the largest reward if it only exploits the acts known. Conversely, if there is too much exploration, then the agent misses taking advantage of what it already learned; it misses fewer but smaller benefits. Thus, the optimal ratio between exploration and exploitation that will make reinforcement learning work needs to be discovered.

Reinforcement learning uses different algorithms. Each of these is designed to work for a particular class of situations and problems. The simplest is Q-learning, an off-policy technique that tries to learn the utility of one particular action within a specific state. The algorithm maintains a Q-table for recording the anticipated utility of every action in every state. The Bellman equation updates Q-values in a table as an agent runs its interactions with the environment and retrieves rewards by using the trade-off between now and future rewards. As it continues interacting with the environment, the agent starts converging towards ideal Q-values where it can make the best choice in differing states. Another widely used on-policy technique is the SARSA (State-Action-Reward-State-Action) algorithm. It is SARSA learning the value of the policy by which the agent acts. This process is different from Q-learning, wherein it learns the best policy irrespective of the actions taken. So, in the process of learning, it implements the behavior policy, and the Q-values are updated based on the actual action that the agent takes in the next phase. This can potentially yield more conservative actions and particularly in applications wherein exploration can lead to side effects.

Another really interesting application is deep reinforcement learning. This is where deep learning and reinforcement learning techniques come together. Traditional reinforcement learning relies on Q-tables or value functions that are usually computationally infeasible for high-dimensional state spaces such as real world applications or complicated games. Deep reinforcement learning approximates the Q-values or even the policy itself using deep neural networks to overcome this limitation. The saga of DeepMind's AlphaGo defeating the human go champions, a combination of reinforcement learning and deep learning, marked an important discovery in the sphere of deep reinforcement learning. This showed how deep reinforcement learning is able to solve complex problems that were prior deemed to be out of the reach of computational powers. A vast array of applications of reinforcement learning are available, so it has a flexibleness and efficiency in respective fields. The most familiar application is in the field of robotics, wherein robots are tested to learn anything through trial and error using reinforcement learning. For instance, it could develop the capabilities such as operating manipulators and using tools and navigation from feedback of actions. It can improve performance by learning optimal policies through simulation of various scenarios until it achieves highly intelligent and autonomous systems.

The second application is that recently reinforcement learning has been significantly used in the gaming industry for designing intelligent agents to be able to play tough games. The one mentioned above, AlphaGo is only an example, and there are other applications of agents in playing first-person shooters or Atari games. These agents result in complex plans and strategies because of the experience they make and can be at par with human performance or even surpass it. This essentially means reinforcement learning in games; it's not only the mark of AI competences but sheds light on how AI systems can be designed to effectively tackle problems in the real world. Reinforcement learning has improved the world of finance significantly. Markets are inherently complex and dynamic, thereby having unpredictability. Algorithms applied in reinforcement learning are more appropriate for risk management, portfolio optimization, and trading strategy. Continuous interaction with real-time market data and adaptation of conditions can improve the strategy of an investor, where RL agents will make their actions more responsive and efficient in achieving maximum gains.

Another interesting application of reinforcement learning occurs in the health sector. RL can be utilized to personalized medicine where the optimal treatment programs for patients can be established by seeing how each patient reacts and with their condition. By scanning the patient's medical history and the alterations in his/her treatment programs, RL algorithms would be able to assess the proper amount of medication that should be given to a patient. Reinforcement learning will also enable health organizations to use their resources appropriately so that service to the patients takes place efficiently in time. Though extremely broad, there has been tremendous success in various application fields through reinforcement learning, but of course, with disadvantages that characterize the objective intended to be achieved in real-world applications. It would require great volumes of interaction data for attaining optimum performance. Such data are likely to be costly and time-consuming to obtain in many practical applications. Furthermore, poorly specified reward functions may give rise to unintended side effects or suboptimal behavior, so one might expect reinforcement learning to be sensitive to the quality of the reward signal. Successful learning is a prerequisite for careful design of incentive structures that work well but are in line with the goals one wants to achieve.

Another challenge is the possibility that agents could be learning undesirable or even dangerous behaviors, especially in highly complex environments. To illustrate, think about a simple example: an agent learning to optimize some objective using RL learns how it can sidestep obstacles or exploit weaknesses in the environment, which have negative impacts. The problem of reward hacking illustrates well the need to design and monitor reinforcement learning systems with care so as to avoid such unexpected consequences. Safety and ethics reinforcement learning is also related to safety and ethics if the domain is sensitive or inherently hazardous, such as healthcare or self-driven systems. It is imperative that RL agents act ethically, and the actions taken by them don't adversely affect people or communities. Researchers are coming up with various ways of applying safety constraints to the algorithms behind reinforcement learning, thus creating effective yet responsible and socially compliant systems.

All this excitement concerning futures full of inventions promises reinforcement learning to keep things rocking. Growth in computing power is also bound to lead toward increasingly more sophisticated and powerful RL algorithms, pushing the frontiers of what can be done. Reinforcement learning combined with other branches of AI, such as computer vision and natural language processing, will produce some powerful hybrids that can tackle complex problems. Perhaps what is exciting about the recent progress in the field of multi-agent reinforcement learning is that this happens by exploring several agents that engage and learn together in the same environment. This seems similar to many real conditions requiring competing or cooperative entities; hence, they are found in social networks, in traffic management, or in supply chains. Multi-agent reinforcement learning is particularly well-suited for developing more robust and flexible systems because agents can learn how to share knowledge among other agents, and since it might adapt its strategies based on the actions of other agents.

With additional development, interpretability and transparency will likely be vital. To instill trust and accountability in critical domains such as health care or finance, one needs to know exactly how the RL agents are making their decisions. Methods for increasing the interpretability of reinforcement learning models are under current investigation in hopes of gaining greater insight into the decision-making processes in such complex systems.

In short, reinforcement learning is an exceptionally strong and dynamic technique of machine learning. Its agents are trained in such a manner to interact with the environment in order to reach the best judgmental decisions. Reinforcement learning has demonstrated its prospects in quite different fields, including both robotics and gaming, finance and healthcare, by reaching an optimal balance between exploration and exploitation in diverse techniques and adapting in diverse applications. There are, however, a number of deeper issues entailed in such use, including not only requirements on the data, safety, and even more abstract questions of morality that must be dealt with. Much remains before the best future for reinforcement learning: the way toward more intelligent, flexible systems that better contend with hard decisions within an increasingly connected world, assuming research continues and technology breakthroughs take place.

## Ethics and Challenges in AI

Artificial intelligence is changing the way people live and work. It brings unprecedented capability and efficiency in domains such as healthcare, banking, transportation, and entertainment. As the technology continues to grow and permeate every walk of life, it beckons a spate of ethical considerations and problems that should be pondered over now. The simple concerns that hang on the first wave of AI advancement include immoral use or biased and discriminatory, privacy issues, accountabilities, and effects on workers and society in general. In essence, this section uses a critical approach to focus on the ethical issues and problems concerning artificial intelligence, with a bias towards the need for developing and implementing AI responsibly and inclusively.

One critical issue with ethics is bias and discrimination through AI. Since AI learns based on data, biased data used for training could actually cause the algorithms to entrain or even exacerbate some preexisting biases within decision-making. For instance, it has been demonstrated that individuals with darker skins have higher error rates compared to facial recognition systems, and this leads to discriminatory impacts for the recruitment and policing process. Also, if the data that the algorithm uses happens to represent biased selection practices, algorithms used in selection processes inadvertently favor membership from certain groups. These outcomes bring questions over the balancer and fairness of such a situation and must open up in AI research and use de-biasing techniques.

Transparency makes AI work fairly and justly. However, most of the algorithms of AI especially deep learning algorithms are viewed as "black boxes" because they are complex and one cannot actually trace back how they come up with some conclusions. Users and stakeholders start losing their trust due to this opaqueness. It will become frustrating and restless to adopt AI-based systems when they do not come to know how the system decides those decisions which affect their life. Therefore, this has been leading to the demands from the practice and research sectors to introduce so-called explainable AI (XAI) methods that will increase the interpretability and friendliness of AI. This then installs confidence in the technology and its outcome when guidelines on what thinking has gone into AI judgment are given.

Another big ethical issue with AI is that of its privacy. Much personal data often collected and analyzed for no apparent reason other than just because AI has been integrated into so many aspects of everyday living. The massive amount of data encompasses everything from social media activities to health records. Relating this data involves fundamental ownership and consent issues regarding how it might be misused, which makes this necessary unless people are sure of their rights, their privacy could be violated because people generally do not know how their information is gathered and used or shared. Apart from this, private information falls into the wrong hands and may even lead to as severe violations as it is a lethal flaw when securing it in the first place. Such issues have to be addressed by organizations through making sure that all the data used is secure and privy to none. They have to make sure that there are robust measures for the protection of data and that the people must be informed and empowered regarding their data.

Another very relevant issue in the ethical standing of AI is accountability. Such systems are becoming more autonomous, that is, they are making choices independently, without human intervention; therefore, the question of who is accountable for the acts of AI systems becomes increasingly complicated. For instance, who should blame in case of an accident that has involved an autonomous car: the manufacturer, its developers, or the car's owner? Knowing whom to place the blame upon also is a prerequisite to solving moral dilemmas because people, or organizations must be taken responsible for the consequences of the AI action. Responsibility is carried not only by people and organizations but also by developers and firms operating AI systems, so respect for moral principles and rules should apply in the very early stages of the development process.

Yet another pressing moral dilemma of which AI will bring about an impact on jobs and employment. This is problematic for a number of industries because, through AI-driven automation, it can eliminate jobs with serious economic and social implications. As AI increases output and opens avenues to work in new ways, others wait, disproportionately affected by this shift: low-skilled occupations. It might be resistance to AI adoption, due to the fear of job loss as a consequence of automation, for instance, or the gap between those who gain from AI breakthroughs and those who do not. There is a need for proactive activities - social safety nets, reskilling and upskilling schemes, and support laws in favor of an inclusive AI deployment strategy. This can be rectified through education and training by empowering their workforce to cope with the changing job environment arising from AI.

The second challenge of ethical AI concerns is the issue of mis/disinformation. AI creates superbly realistic content, for example, deepfakes and synthetic media, which raises questions about the quantity of bad content that could be circulated. The rise of disinformation campaigns hinging on AI will gradually erode public trust in institutions and the media, push society to even greater polarization, and destabilize communities. The problem thus reveals the need to establish certain frameworks of morality and of law governing the use of AI in communication and in media. Correct practices from the supporters would extend the credibility of information and minimize most of the risks that are related to this false data.

There's no way to ignore the influence that AI makes upon the entire world. The existing gaps in accessible access and requirements between the countries or even regions may become more significant as AI technologies spread. More developed countries that have better technological advancements will probably reap more of the positive impacts of developments in AI, while poorer nations are lagging behind because they are still trying to catch up. This injustice may call for the representation and participation question in the development or use of AI. It is in the universal access of AI technology across all geographic and financial boundaries that ensures progress in terms of greater international equity and mutual benefits. International cooperation and the sharing of knowledge may be very important in resolving these differences and creating a much fairer environment of AI.

Many pro-advocates include academics, decision-makers, and business executives who are pushing for moral frameworks and standards that must guide the development of artificial intelligence. The ideas of justice, accountability, transparency, and privacy reemerged in initiatives such as the European Commission AI Ethics

Guidelines and the OECD Principles on Artificial Intelligence. Such principles offer a foundation upon which to build ethical AI technology and, thereby enhance public trust in their use. The second is interdisciplinary collaboration. Indeed, the multidisciplinary approach of computer science, philosophy, sociology, and law will provide more holistic form of analysis on the ethics of artificial intelligence. An interdisciplinary setup involving ethicists, scholars, and practitioners may hence have the chance to expose the dilemmas likely to arise in dealing with ethical issues, explore innovative solutions, and make sure that artificial intelligence technologies align with the values of society.

It means that knowledge and consciousness of the issues regarding AI ethical matters would be quintessential. All the more, it is crucial to have the public brought up to speed regarding the ethical questions raised by AI and its implications as more and more technologies of this kind infuse into daily life. This would give people better insight into the niceties of AI technology in making intelligent decisions on how to utilize them. In this regard, it can spur on the developers and practitioners to develop an ethical-oriented culture that enforces responsible behaviors in AI development, offering a sense of accountability. Good regulatory frameworks show significant ethical issues of AI. Governance and regulation require timely clarity from governments and regulatory bodies on definition and standards for AI research and application, which can well incorporate ethical issues at all phases of the lifecycle of an AI system. Polices of fairness, accountability, and openness also help mitigate risks while ensuring the protection of rights of individuals to innovate in the AI industry.

Such fast development in the arena of artificial intelligence has raised rather serious ethical issues that have to be addressed within a fair and responsible framework. All the way from employment to misinformation, transparency to privacy, accountability to bias, and global imbalances, these issues raise a call for an overarching approach to AI ethics. Therefore, for a technologically efficient AI-based landscape, the appropriate mix of ethical frameworks must be available, interdisciplinary cooperation encouraged, better education and awareness created, and effective regulatory measures in place so that society can reap its fruits within the shackles of individual liberty and social mores as it continues to march forward only after the ethical issues of AI are addressed. the way to ethical AI, not a strictly technological issue nor just a moral one but a combination of all the efforts of parties, which may have an influence on shaping the development of technology.

# CHAPTER V

# Data Visualization and Storytelling

## The Power of Data Visualization

Data has penetrated all dimensions of modern society and infused decision-making in government, industry, healthcare, and education. As the volume of data being collected is increasing exponentially with time, gathering, evaluating, and finally, successfully presenting insights gained from the data becomes increasingly difficult. Data visualization now allows people and organizations to communicate complex information as intelligible, relevant, and convenient. Data visualization is an opportunity wherein people will be in a position to assist many people within different stakeholder groups to understand concepts, recognize patterns, and make informed decisions through the creation of pictures such as maps, graphs, and charts.

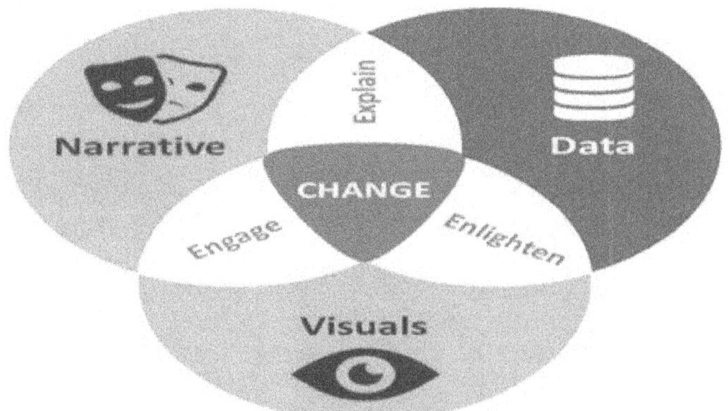


Value of Data Visualization, Benefits Key Principles, Good Visual Communication, Tools and Techniques, Leveraging the Power of Data Visualization, Graphical Representation of Information and Data. The graphics-representational component of data visualization is the graphical representation of information and data. Data visualization permits apparently complex data sets to be grasped and understood in greater terms by using colors, shapes, and patterns. It is well known that the human brain takes less time to process visual information than written information. It has been scientifically proven that images are digested 60,000 times faster than words. Visual communication is, therefore, a very effective means of transferring information between people. It basically speaks to the fact that in today's data-driven world, data visualization plays such an important role in the sense that it becomes crucially important for the effectiveness and clarity of communication.

This is one of the most noticeable benefits: the capacity of data visualization to take complicated information and make it clearer. The challenge that faces stakeholders in this data world is making sense of enormous volumes of data,. Visualizations thus ease complexity and allow users to see anomalies, correlations, or trends in raw data largely unseen. For instance, a big consumer preference dataset stretched over various categories of demographics can be taken as an example. A set of data visualization tools was used to construct an interactive dashboard with filters and interactive data exploration for use by stakeholders. More profound underlying patterns in data are graphically explained through interactivity, thus making it possible for organizations to make proper informed decisions based on data.

Deepening data-driven storytelling: Data visualization also deepens data-driven storytelling. Facts mixed with appealing images of the eyes entwine to weave compelling tales when narration is the factor producing opinion and choice. Organizations can explain their research through a story by contextualizing data and taking the observer through all of the nitty-gritty while highlighting a point of interest, such as non-profits raising consciousness about a social issue so that they can communicate how their work has impacted society and just how far they have come with time through nice charts and infographics. Data visualization is of great importance as it is part of advocacy and communication because it will enable organizations to elicit emotions and inspire action by narrating a story through the data.

Among the most highly effective features of modern data visualization is interaction. Advanced visualization tools have been designed that allow stakeholders to explore the data dynamically, and thus, it provides a much more individualized experience. Interactive visualizations allow users to filter, zoom, and drill down into the data to provide deeper insights customized to the needs of the user. A healthcare company can create an interactive dashboard that enables the customers to investigate patient outcomes based on different treatment modalities or demographics. At this stage, interactivity incites participation as stakeholders are empowered to locate specific information that is peculiar to their problems or subject of interest.

In the recent past, many tools and technologies have been developed to make data visualization better and available to everyone. More complexity to this, even traditional tools like Excel or PowerPoint find space when simple visualizations are at consideration, and on the side-by-side continuum with Tableau or Power BI or D3.js. In addition, the tools utilize intuitive interfaces that a user can exploit toward creating more complex visualizations without having to learn much about programming. These free tools have become necessities for any data scientists and analysts to come up with unique visualizations based on their datasets and concerns of research. The advent of AI and machine learning has revolutionized the data visualization process. Such visualization can be automated by AI-driven technologies that will best propose a chart for the data being analyzed. This saves time, improves accuracy, and the algorithm is more capable of discovering patterns and trends than a human analyst is. However, placing the machine learning models into the visualizations will allow the stakeholders to compare projections and predictions side-by-side with their historical data for proper understanding of the data landscape.

Data visualization has so many advantages, yet there are still challenges that prevent its effective implementation. For instance, they can manipulate or misrepresent the data by the use of misleading displays. This amount of power in visualization means that data must, therefore, be represented in an honest and ethical manner. Stakeholders must watch out for cherry-picking of data, scaling manipulation, or use of misleading visuals. False representations can cause much trouble by giving spurious inferences. This will be so vital for public policy as well as health care: wrong decisions taken on the basis of data may have huge repercussions in a person's life.

The other challenge is that data literacy among stakeholders is necessary. Though data visualization technologies are becoming increasingly ubiquitous, good interpretation of visualization has at base a basic understanding of the concepts of data. Employer focus on training and education should be a strong, developing data literacy in employees so that they may communicate with data visualizations and make invaluable inferences from them. A data literacy culture may also enable the organizations in their efforts toward visualization of data and making informed decisions. Discussion ideas on ethics issues in data visualization: With every other concern posted on data security and privacy, one cannot very well neglect the ethical dimensions of data visualization. In this regard, businesses must be careful with the potential impacts of visualizing sensitive data so that one's privacy or confidentiality is not ever compromised. The fact that data is made anonymous and the use of informed consent as well as awareness of the respective laws are critical measures to ensure that ethics in data visualization are brought into being. Organizations should also produce visually inclusive and accessible visualizations where considerations are taken into account for the richness of audiences as well as their levels of data literacy.

Thus, data visualization is a great business communication tool due to its ability to facilitate communication of complicated information to stakeholders. It makes for knowledge of the subject matter, cooperation, and well-informed decisions that prove priceless. With raw data capable of representing graphical format, the stakeholders might discover patterns or trends or insights that would have been lost in writing. In this regard, associated benefits include a better narrative, better participation by stakeholders, and better clarity. All of which have to be cleared first, together with ethical questions the application brings in its wake, then etiquette of good visual communication and integration of leading-edge tools and technology; for all this data visualization to be applied inappropriately. As long as data is going to remain an important aspect in the shaping of our environment, the power of data visualization is going to prove crucial for developing in-depth analysis and fostering data-driven decision-making for many industries. Much awaits in the future of data visualization, where it shall continue offering opportunities to advance our understanding of the complexities of our data-intensive environments while maintaining moral considerations in the design and application of data visualizations.


## Telling a Compelling Data Story

It is fundamental to convey insights during the big data era. Companies and individuals are surrounded by data, and they need it transformed into meaningful insights that make data storytelling such an amazing tool. The technique applies both data analysis and narrative for crafting compelling stories in informing and inspiring. Understanding the data and the audience launches such tellers to craft the most engaging data stories that elicit meaningful answers. It speaks of data storytelling, which is the narrative in data display, and tactics that can lead one to take action in a data store.

Data storytelling refers to the process of telling a clear and compelling narrative from raw data. It begins with finding a clear message or insight from the data. The process involves data examination and requires an understanding of context. Context is relevant to the interpretation of data. A quarter-long sales decline will seem ominous. Stakeholders will be misled by data if it contains information about seasonal variations or economic trends. Storytellers can help listeners understand what they are supposed to hear by putting data into context. Having made a main point, sound data narrative should possess a superior narrative structure. Data stories, like all stories, should have a beginning, middle, and end. The situation and the problem are introduced in the beginning part, which grabs the attention of the audience right away. The middle part consists of the statistics as well as analysis to back up the story. Visuals facilitate understanding and engagement here. Charts, graphs, and infographics make complex data simple through patterns, comparisons, and correlations. Critical findings should explain in data insights actionable suggestions. Such a structure makes the story flow logically and easier to understand.

Narrative plays a core role in data storytelling. Humankind is fascinating in stories; they permit us to say, know, and connect. Presenters can invoke emotions and capture people in by placing data in a framework of the story. Providing a relation between the story and people forms the foundation for the increased probability of action towards insights achieved by discovering this finding. A health care company may exploit patient results as a strategy to connect these to human accounts and how therapy changed their life. Humanizing data enables an organization to find ways of presenting the findings and convincing their investors to invest in more research or implementation.

Effective data storytelling also needs audience understanding and even the adaptation of a story. Data users would be different regarding their acquaintance with data, what's of interest to them, and what is motivating. A technical audience is interested in techniques and statistical significance, but a non-technical audience will demand more visualization and accessible anecdotes. Story adaptation increases audience engagement and message delivery. This audience-centric approach makes stakeholders feel connected to the insights created and accountable for it.

That is an important understanding of the audience and media for a data story. Presentations, reports, videos, and dashboards for interactive input open up huge possibilities for engagement and interaction. Each of these mediums has pros and cons. The format should be in-line with the goals as well as the preferences of the audience of the presentation. The live presentations help when the interests are interactive with the presenters in real-time and input while the well-designed reports give a complete overview for further study. Optical media will enrich the data storytelling, bringing the right information and communication of insight. Data storytelling would naturally include visualization. Used properly, visualization makes the content easier to understand, implies trends, and has the ability to draw the attention of the audience. However, graphics should be used judiciously. Too many pictures and a poorly designed presentation of graphics can overpower the listener's ability to hear a story. Instead, presenters should make it easier and more comprehensible. A restricted color palette and a uniform font can be part of it. Then, of course, there's the need to label chart and graph axes properly. Visual analogues also enable the audience to envision a project timeline, such as a road map with the flow of events and milestones.

Qualitative data should be integrated with the quantitative data to make effective data storytelling. The former has numerical evidence, but the latter has personal testimonials, expert opinions, and anecdotes, giving depth and perspective; hence, giving the storyteller a much clearer view of the topic in question. A business measuring customer satisfaction may have the ability to illustrate survey data and testimony from customers who received great or noteworthy service. The more interesting and accessible the story with both quantitative and qualitative data it reveals, the more human effect to the numbers and more ineluctable action. A compelling call to action must accompany action by data story. At the end of findings, describe next actions. A clear call to action guides stakeholders to invest in a new venture, change a marketing strategy, or change policy. This segment of the data story connects insight to action: stakeholders are educated on the data but encouraged to act on it at the same time. The nonprofit presenting efficacy program results is likely to end with an appeal for funding for next projects. The audience can fund and lobby by customizing the narrative in a tangible ask.

Facts may become inaccurate and misleading if data is manipulated or suppressed. Such implications can be avoided if the data storyteller explains the sources, methods, and constraints of the data. This makes the transparency thereby increase audience confidence and credibility in the insight. A culture of ethical data storytelling in businesses promotes responsible actions and reduction in misrepresentation. A data story can break into action and illuminate decision-making in a world full of data. Stakeholders can be engaged, emotions evoked, and action triggered if raw data is transformed into storytelling. Understanding the audience is number one; knowing how to organize the story is the second; and using visuals as an aid to comprehension is the third. Data storytelling is a narrative crafting that speaks to the human impact of data and uses statistical and non-statistical insights. Of course, clear calls to action and the rich appeal would also motivate stakeholders into acting on the insights. As long as technology continues to improve, there would be a constant demand for data storytelling to make a change through application in organizations. In that regard, data literacy and ethical storytelling are a must soon to help organizations make the most of what their data story has to offer and make sagacious judicious decisions among stakeholders.

# CONCLUSION

As we close in on the end of "Unlocking Data Insights: Mastering Data Science for Impact: Harnessing Big Data for Smarter Decisions," it is clear that data science has taken a far greater role in the day-to-day decision-making processes for all modern firms than ever before. We have discussed the revolutionary potential of big data and machine learning and how to apply them toward driving innovation, optimizing workflow, and unearthing important insights.

With this book, you now know how to command everything in the data science process-from advanced modeling and visualization all the way through data preparation and collection. Wherever you work and whatever your level of experience, the practical methods, case studies, and best practices presented throughout will help you apply data science concepts to real-world problems.

However, that is not the end of the adventure. The world of data science is, of course, constantly changing, and keeping on top of things requires continuous education and adaptability. Your ability to exploit data will continue to grow with new tools, algorithms, and ethical issues arising.

The purpose of this book is to arm you with the ability to make decisions of real-world impact using data. You can incorporate these skills with a data-driven attitude to turn data into an asset that can help you uncover insights potentially powerful sufficiently to shape your business or personal goals in the future. The potential is limitless, and now it's ready to be unleashed.